The Fat Adapted Running Formula™

A Step-by-Step Guide to Becoming a Fat Adapted Runner

By:
Michael D'Aulerio

When every step of your run begins to feel like the first step of your run, you have mastered fat adapted running.

The Fat Adapted Running Formula™
Copyright © 2019 by Michael D'Aulerio.
All rights reserved.

For information about this title or to order other books and/or electronic media, contact the publisher:

Long Run Living LLC
longrunliving@gmail.com
http://www.LongRunLiving.com
Printed in the USA

Disclaimer

Table of Contents

PREFACE:

Start Here

There is a near-infinite source of sustainable energy in each and every one of us. It's a goldmine, it's free, and it's extractable for any runner who aspires to run extraordinary distances. Although it exacts a toll on both mind and body, since it demands a new mindset, you'll receive in the end a devised strategy with a unique approach to running.

Many runners today still remain unmindful and uninformed of this most abundant source of energy. They are far too occupied searching for external forms of fuel, rather than internal sources. The constant allure to the next magic pill, fabled elixir, or mythical fountain are non-existent and without merit. Yet their search continues, maintaining the validity of the proverbial shortcut that doesn't exist. Even the so-called short-term or quick fix is short-lived at best.

External forms of energy, such as performance-enhancing supplements like gels, sports drinks, powders, and bars are beneficial to a degree, but at what cost? Is breaking the bank and chancing detrimental or potential side effects worth it? Especially since these products commonly produce minimal results. Some runners supplement to improve running, increase endurance, or maintain a consistent body weight. Yet as stated, most external sources of energy fall short of their guarantees. Time wasted, money spent, and possible adverse effects are just a few of the many downsides to the supplement industry's promises.

There are enormous forms of eternal energy and supplementation flooding the market every day and yet all the power you could ever want or need comes from within. Not from supplements nor magic, and most definitely it doesn't happen overnight. In fact, specific steps must be taken to acclimate your mind, body, and soul, so it is more able to tap into this internal and most plentiful source of energy.

The source of energy I am referring to is *stored body fat*. By following the guidelines in this book of fact-proven methods, you too could become quite efficient at burning fat for fuel.

The Fat Adapted Running Formula™ will have you running further with less effort. You'll also regulate weight control, eliminate sugar cravings, and at the same time become a healthier you. All while saving money in the process. How's that sound? Great, I hope.

So who created *The Fat Adapted Running Formula*™? I did and my name is Michael D'Aulerio. Besides being an author, I'm also a super-passionate ultramarathon runner. Maybe a super-obsessive ultrarunner is a better way of stating it! I've run over 100 ultra distances within a handful of years. I've run 50ks, 50 miles, 100ks, 100 miles and 116 miles across the state of Florida. I've even run one of the longest ultramarathons in the world: 200 miles.

Fat adaptation was the game changer for me. So much so, in fact, I now run for prolonged periods of time and distances up to and including a 50k ultramarathon entirely without food or water.

Marathon running was once a dream, but now, just another day of speed training. Ultramarathons were once an impossibility, but now...a way of life. Those words may be the truest words ever spoken, and yet the following words are true as well: if I can do it, so can you!

Through fat adapted running, any distance is possible for anyone if they're willing to commit to the work. If followed correctly, you too will discover the secret to becoming a fat adapted runner. The secret that's from within and most definitely not from outside sources. The best news of all is that I share the entire process of becoming fat adapted in this book, called *The Fat Adapted Running Formula*™. Each page will guide you from a beginner to a fat adapted running machine in a few and easy-to-follow steps.

Within each chapter, you'll receive several tips designed to propel you through your fat adapted running journey. At the same time, I understand not everyone will follow every step of every chapter—well guess what? That's OK! However, the closer you follow the formula, the more promising your results will be. Feel free to use this book as your guide or a blueprint. Take the "a la carte" approach or follow it diligently. The choice is yours.

If I could offer only one piece of advice during your fat adapted running journey it's this: LISTEN TO YOUR BODY. Paying attention to how your body responds to the upcoming changes will help you make the best nutritional choices along the way. A nutritious choice for one runner may vary slightly from another. So it's critical to listen to your own body the entire time. For example, I recommend cutting out grains from your diet entirely. This made a huge difference in my progression towards becoming fat adapted. From experience I know it will be a game changer for most beginners, and although it's a useful measure to take, not all fat adapted runners follow this advice. Some eat a small portion of grains daily but they make sure it's low in starch. So, again, follow *The Fat Adapted Running Formula*™, but listen to your body.

Understand this: what you put into fat adapted running is exactly what you get out. If you make radical changes in your diet, then you will see radical changes in your body. Likewise, if your commitment to fat adapted running is minimal, then your gains will be minimal, and trust me, the difference is apparent.

For instance, you may go through weeks of near perfection. Your diet seems flawless. You'll practice running with no food or water, and your body will start burning fat as fuel efficiently, but then…you decide to go out for a night and let loose. After a night of pizza, cake, and alcohol, you wake up and go for a run. A few miles into training you notice a big difference. You feel the negative effects of deviating from *The Fat Adapted Running Formula*™. Now, your body is demanding a sports drink or gel much earlier than usual in your run. Unfortunately, you've just taken a few steps backward and must start moving forward again. No, you don't fall back to square one, but you certainly lose momentum.

Understand there are no finish lines to fat adapted running. You either become more efficient at burning fat or less. There's not a static position to fat adaptation, though there are rewards for your hard work. You see, the more efficient you become at burning fat, the longer it takes to lose that efficiency. So try your best to stay on course, especially in the beginning.

Soon you won't want to sacrifice your progress for that piece of cake. The euphoria you feel on a daily basis will not be worth the night out. The key is to reach that threshold of no return. To do so, at the beginning of your training, requires a diligent effort.

Another critical point to emphasize is how this book is for all levels of running. Whether you've run a 5k, 10k, half-marathon, marathon, or ultramarathon, there's a tailored plan for you. The only prerequisite is to be a human being with a working metabolism, and since everyone who reads this book is indeed human, then yes—this book is for you!

Can you imagine what life feels like as a fat adapted runner? Picture yourself waking up before every training run and walking straight out the door. No more timing a pre-run meal. No more chugging down sports drinks. No more stuffing your pockets full of gels. No more upset stomach. Just a healthy body, running shoes, and the open road. What an incredible experience running will become. Or imagine shedding off that 10, 20, or 30 extra pounds from training your body to efficiently burn its own fat as fuel, and not only does the fat burn off…it stays off. You now feel light on your feet and have developed a lean runner's body—you know, that slim yet muscular body so many of us long for but can't figure out how to develop. Visualize your new lean runner's body in the mirror. What an amazing transformation. Then see yourself crossing the finish line of that marathon or ultramarathon. You know, that distance you've been secretly planning to run but can't find a clear path to get there. Do you understand what happens to a person who completes a race of such magnitude? How their running changes? How their life changes?

Fat adapted running will demolish that self-created sugar-induced wall. That wall stopping you from reaching longer distances. That wall that cripples your progress due to a sugar dependency. Yes, you knock down the dreaded wall, allowing you to run any distance imaginable. Then you not only cross the finish line but you *become* that person who can cross the finish line. Running a marathon or ultramarathon will not only improve your running, but it will also improve your life. Fat adapted running makes it all possible.

If you're ready to run extraordinary distances, become a minimalist runner, and drop a few pounds in the process, then keep reading *The Fat Adapted Running Formula*™. Before we get started, let's discuss how to read this book.

Please note: I am not a certified nutritionist and make no claims to the contrary. You are ultimately responsible for all decisions pertaining to your health. Remember, sometimes when you push the limits, the limits push back. So, proceed with caution and never forget that safety comes first.

How to Read This Book

The Fat Adapted Running Formula™ starts with an introduction to fat adapted running and an explanation of its benefits, followed by a breakdown for each part of the equation:

Fat Adapted Running = The Foundation + The Bridge + The Transformation + The Calibration + The Glue

The Foundation is designed to adjust your lens to see a new scope of nutrition. No, you won't find food pyramids and serving sizes in this chapter. Instead, it's packed with practical nutritional tips to prepare your body for fat adapted running. *The Foundation* alone has the potential to transform your body completely and provide extraordinary energy for your running. However, the purpose of this book provides the foundation to becoming a fat adapted runner.

The Bridge is also about nutrition, but this chapter is what guides you from being a healthy runner to one who burns fat as fuel. *The Foundation* provides many tips to choose from, and not all are required to follow; however, *The Bridge* offers crucial tips that are highly recommended. They may seem extreme to some, but looking at fat adaptation as a whole, they are the few small yet necessary steps required for transformation. These critical steps, if followed, will make the fat adapted transformation happen quicker.

The Transformation brings you from a fat adapted person to a fat adapted runner. It's the mechanics, the nuts and bolts. It's the chapter on running—more specifically, running on empty. Based on your skill level, you choose one out of the five training programs to follow. In the end, and in unison with your new nutritional habits, you'll have become a fat adapted runner. Here is where your body becomes much more efficient at burning fat as fuel. Again, what you invest into fat adapted running is what you reap. So if you take *The Transformation* to its extreme, you will have made extreme progress.

The Calibration is where we dial-in your new fat adapted body. I will provide a natural approach to becoming more fat adapted. *The Calibration* chapter is optional but with enough effort, it will take your fat adapted running to the next level. Here is where you will increase your pace or progress to further distances in a shorter period of time. So feel free to use *The Calibration* chapter as much or as little as you'd like. It all depends on your goals and how your body feels.

Once you have completed *The Foundation, The Bridge, The Transformation,* and *The Calibration*, you will have finished the physical side of *The Fat Adapted Running Formula*™. I will then walk you through the last step: *The Glue*.

The Glue is what holds the entire formula together: your mindset. Within this chapter, I offer a new way of thinking for developing a fat adapted running mindset. You begin to understand how fat adapted running is a lifestyle. Yes, it requires a change in your body, but it also requires a change in your mind.

Afterward, you can then take a deep breath…and welcome yourself home. You'll now have a normal human metabolism.

Remember this: the process of becoming a fat adapted runner can take months. This means you can expect to come back to *The Fat Adapted Running Formula*™ several times. In fact, I highly recommend it. I can't tell you how many times I've reread something only to gain even more insight the second time. You may have missed something the first time or because of your progress, read it again but from a new mindset or a new perspective. As you become fat adapted, each day will be different from the last. Your running changes, your body changes and your mind changes. So each time you come back to this book, you'll be reading as a new runner. A new runner with new strengths and new adversities to overcome.

My advice is to read *The Foundation* and make incremental changes each day. Truly focus on building your foundation. With this chapter in mind, you can jump right into *The Bridge*. Make the changes within this chapter immediately. Even if the changes aren't perfect, make them to the best of your abilities. Don't let an obsession for perfection prevent you from making progress.

Once you made the changes from *The Bridge,* move forward. Start the running programs immediately in *The Transformation* chapter and tweak your new dietary changes from *The Foundation* and *The Bridge* as you go. Do this, and you're on a direct path to becoming a fat adapted machine.

As you read *The Calibration* chapter, you will have a decision to make. You can either (A) wait until you finish your running program from *The Transformation* before starting; or (B), begin *The Calibration* chapter halfway through your new running program. This will be a decision you make based on how your body feels.

By the time you reach *The Glue*, you will be ready to develop a fat adapted runner mindset. By gaining a deeper meaning for your fat adapted running journey, you will find purpose in your actions, and a person with purpose is an unbreakable one.

Understand that although *The Fat Adapted Running Formula*™ provides incredible results, we all have different bodies. Some of the nutritional tips that work for one person may not work for another. So let me remind you again: LISTEN TO YOUR BODY. When you eat a particular way, or at a certain time, be aware of how it affects your body and how your energy feels. At the same time, don't let crippling excuses prevent you from making effective changes along the way. Because I know this for sure: if you look for excuses…you'll always find them

Today is the day you start focusing on your energy. You focus on where it's coming from, where it's going and how it makes you feel. So, listen to your body and start diving into each chapter. Welcome yourself to the world of fat adapted running. A place where some of the greatest athletes on the planet reside…and soon…a place you will call home. Let's burn some fat!

INTRODUCTION:

A Fat Fueling Journey

When every step of your run begins to feel like the first step of your run, you have mastered fat adapted running. That's the best way I can explain becoming a fat adapted runner. After running 31 miles (50k) with no food or water, I discovered just how incredible fat adapted running was. However, I must warn you, becoming a fat adapted runner takes hard work. It takes a consistent effort and a constant intention in fine-tuning your fat metabolism. Yes, you can implement the formula I teach you and turn into a fat adapted runner. However, fat adapted running challenges you both physically and mentally. So prepare yourself mentally to make these lifestyle changes.

Becoming a fat adapted runner takes you a step backward, but once you start the challenge, the results are astonishing. Your body transforms, and the results are apparent whether viewed from the mirror or in your running shoes. Your body transforms. It's unbelievable. Personally, I now leave my house with zero supplies during all my training runs under 40 miles. So unless I'm training for a 100-mile ultramarathon or longer, I'm running on empty. There are weight loss benefits as well. Not only did I cut an extra 15-20 lbs off my running weight, but a high-fat diet provides more energy throughout your day. The energy is long lasting and sustainable, and as long as you have the fat in your body, then it will use it as fuel.

But running didn't always feel so great for me. The reason I began fat adapted running wasn't just an idea, it was a solution to a big problem I was experiencing. You see, when I first began ultramarathon running, every race led to an upset, nauseated stomach. Even with how challenging ultramarathons are, I fell in love with the sport, but those challenges got worse before they got better. During every single race, nausea would come like clockwork at the 25-30 mile mark. Nausea would then intensify, haunting me for the rest of the race. I would then find myself curled up on the couch shortly after. I needed to fix this problem…and fast. The thought of not running another ultramarathon was heartbreaking.

Eventually, I realized the nausea was from the excess sugars I ate before, during, and after races. My carbo-loading strategy was completely outdated, and my body knew it. It was an explosive sugary massacre, and my stomach was the victim. So, after a whole lot of trial and error, I eliminated *all* processed foods from my life. Here's the thing: most processed foods contain large amounts of sugar. I began eating a diet rich in good fats and upped my intake of green leafy vegetables.

I also began fueling all-natural. No more gels, sports drinks, bars, blocks, or any other performance supplements. I went back to the ultimate expert in performance and well-being herself: Mother Nature. This not only changed my running for the better…it changed my life. Eating all-natural and eliminating foods like grains, dairy, and processed food naturally reduced my sugars. Then increasing my consumption of essential oils and nuts and seeds added more good fats to my diet.

So, as you now know, it was nausea that led me to research fat adapted running and implement it into my life. Not only did it cure my issue with nausea but I morphed into a runner who can run long distances with minimal sustenance. I began listening to my body, and eventually…it naturally led me to a high-fat lifestyle. I even became plant-based and stopped eating meat—so vegetarians, fat adapted running is an option for you too.

What I can say is none of my dietary choices are forever. I've just let my body dictate my eating habits as I run further and further as an endurance runner. Maybe one day it will take me down another path. For now, I eat a high-fat diet and have learned the art of fat adapted running.

So now that you know my story, it's time to create yours. First, for those who don't understand what fat adapted running is, allow me to explain. Keep reading as I discuss the essence of fat adapted running and the problems that come along with being a sugar-dependent runner.

CHAPTER 1:

What Is Fat Adapted Running?

Now that you know who I am and my story, the question becomes, "What is fat adapted running?" You may have heard terms like "fat as fuel," "fat adapted running," or even "the keto diet" thrown around, but they all refer to a high-fat diet. Although it's not really a "diet" at all, just a new way of eating. Remember—it's not a diet change, it's a *lifestyle* change that's required. Change the way you eat and change your life forever.

So how does a high-fat diet actually work? What is fat adaptation? The process of fat adaptation refers to moving your body's primary energy source from glucose (sugar) to fatty acids (fat). When this occurs, your body stops depending on sugars (carbs) and prefers fat as fuel instead. Your body becomes far more efficient in burning its own stored fat as fuel and is less dependent on sugar. Low sugar, in a perfect world, means no sugar crash, no constant replenishment, and no sugar addiction. Just a continuous flow of sustainable energy, available to you always. As you can imagine, this comes in handy during periods of prolonged running.

When your body is efficient at burning fat as fuel, you can run longer without needing to refuel because the fuel comes from within. Fat adaptation is the body's preferred metabolic state. That's what our bodies are designed to do. We eat, store fat, and use it for energy later.

Okay, so you may be asking yourself...What about sugar (carbs)? Shouldn't runners eat carbs for energy? And that's an excellent question. So, to understand better, let's take a look at a sugar-dependent runner.

The Sugar-Dependent Runner

Runners who depend on sugar are incredibly inefficient at burning fat as fuel. So their body's only other option is to burn glucose (sugar). This makes them reliant on carbs and sugar when they run, and if they run long enough without it, they crash hard. So when a runner "hits the wall," the brain is actually shutting the muscles down in order to conserve sugar for the nervous system.

However, when you are efficient at burning fat as fuel, there is no wall. Your body has plenty of energy to go around. The average body contains much more fat than it does sugar. So once you can efficiently burn fat as fuel, you tap into an enormous supply of energy. That's opposed to burning sugar as fuel, which burns fast, and must be replenished regularly.

So if a runner primarily burns sugar as fuel, they can't stay in a fasted state without experiencing extreme fatigue. A sugar-dependent runner will be unable to benefit from the advantages of fat adapted running. The advantages I'm referring to are more sustainable energy, longer mileage, and healthy weight loss. This leaves sugar burners with only a few options...and they aren't pretty: constantly eating, consistently hungry, burning more food but less fat, and even poor hormonal imbalance.

Please note, in theory, the body uses both fatty acids (fat) and glucose (sugar) for energy but never at the same time. The type of fuel the body uses is regulated by its hormones (insulin) which are regulated mainly by the food you eat (carbs, fat, protein). Remember—insulin is produced whenever your blood glucose (sugar) levels extend over a set threshold. Briefly summarized: when insulin is available, you burn glucose. When insulin is unavailable, you burn fat.

How to Escape the Sugar Bowl

Do you feel stuck as a sugar-dependent runner? Don't worry…there's a way out. If you follow *The Fat Adapted Running Formula*™, I will be throwing you a lifesaver from the sugary pit of constant fatigue. I will pull you out onto the other side where some of the greatest endurance athletes in the world reside.

Are you ready to jump out of the sugar bowl for good? The way out is through fat adapted running. To help better serve you, I will explain my formula for becoming a fat adapted runner. It's a formula you won't find in any other books. This process is from my hands-on experience. As a fat adapted runner I've run…

- over 100 ultramarathon distances
- 40 miles with no food or water
- numerous 50ks with no food or water
- nausea away from my ultramarathon career
- 15-20 lbs off my race weight
- several 100-mile races
- 116 miles across the state of Florida
- one of the longest distances in the world: 200 miles

Will becoming fat adapted guarantee similar results? No, but will it provide the *opportunity* to achieve similar results? Absolutely!

So, as you can see, fat adapted running has its advantages. Once you become a fat adapted runner, it's up to you to maintain your new superpowers. What effects those powers the most is what you're doing when you're *not* running. It's about how true you can stick to a healthy lifestyle.

One last thing before jumping into the benefits of fat adapted running. I always learn best with analogies, so if it helps, here's one for burning sugar versus fat as fuel. Burning fat is like burning coal: slow and steady, burning and burning for a long time. Conversely, sugar is like lighter fluid, a quick flash, then POOF...it's gone. So, when you're trying to reach longer distances, especially ultramarathon distances, which type of fire do you want to burn?

If you're ready to burn some coal, that is, ready to burn fat as fuel, then keep reading forward and start your fat adapted running journey today.

CHAPTER 2:

The Benefits of Fat Adapted Running

Becoming a fat burning machine provides enormous benefits. I've splashed several self-transformative advantages throughout this book already. So by now, I think it's safe to say fat adapted running can help you run further distances, but is that all it can do? Is improving your long run the only benefit? The answer: far from it. The benefits of fat adapted running stretch far beyond clocking miles. A high-fat running lifestyle also comes with an avalanche of positive lifestyle changes. Everything from losing weight to helping with disease are the gifts you receive as a fat adapted runner. If done correctly, it will provide an explosion of sustainable energy that lasts all day.

I'm getting ahead of myself. There are a handful of extraordinary advantages you will take away from fat adapted running. So read on as I discuss each benefit as well as how they will improve your running and your life.

Running Becomes Easier

One day, running a marathon was an impossible feat. At one time, I couldn't comprehend covering a distance of such magnitude. Now I consider it a short run. I've even gone on to run eight consecutive marathons during a single race. Yes, fat adaptation was a contributing factor that helped me run a 200-mile ultramarathon. No, fat adaptation alone will not push you across the finish line in a race of such unfathomable lengths, but it sure helps, and in a big way.

I've run 100-mile ultramarathons as a sugar-dependent runner, and I've run them as a fat adapted runner. So trust me when I tell you that there's a clear difference between the two. Fat adapted running makes the experience much more manageable, and you know what? It makes it much more enjoyable as well.

What makes the difference? In other words, why does running become easier? Well, there are several factors. Studies have shown that fat adapted runners have more mitochondria, a lower lactate load, and lower oxidative stress. Also, fat adapted runners can function at much higher intensity while burning fat. The result: running becomes easier. Can you imagine the possibilities? Do you see the potential of burning fat as fuel efficiently? It's like dropping a more powerful engine inside the body of your car. Except it's your actual body and you are transforming the engine from within instead of swapping it out. In addition, your new body prefers the new fuel to run on—meaning, it prefers fats, good quality fats.

I'm sure I don't have to tell you fat adapted running will improve your endurance and make running easier. The fact that you are reading this book demonstrates your belief. It's no secret, and it's available to everyone who is willing to apply the effort.

Fat adapted brings more efficiency to your running thus allowing you to move faster and further. It may be the extra edge you've been looking for. Or...it may be the transformative life changer you've been praying for. Either way, you can start your fat adapted running journey today.

Fat Melts Away

Do you run and hope to lose weight, but can't figure out how? Does it seem like your weight stays the same no matter how much you run? Are you tired of seeing no results on the scale?

If you answered "yes" to any of those questions, then guess what? You're not alone. You're experiencing the same frustrations as most sugar-dependent runners. The fact is, most runners fail at losing weight because they are sugar dependent. Their bodies aren't efficient at burning fat.

What some runners don't realize is that sugar—if not used for energy—eventually stores as body fat. Furthermore, since sugar is so addictive, hence the term "sugar craving," it forces you to overeat, thus storing more fat. I will discuss this process in greater depth in a later chapter.

Simply put, if your body is dependent on sugar, then it's terrible at burning fat. Conversely, when your body primarily burns fat as fuel, it becomes excellent at burning fat. Make sense? As a fat adapted runner, not only are you burning more fat, but you're reducing sugar cravings. That's because your body begins to prefer good fats to function. Over time, you can go longer without eating and run further without fuel.

Get the point? It's a very basic explanation, but it's a very basic process. Don't let the details scare you from making a change—a change that will transform your life. Eventually, your body weight spirals downwards and you knock off that extra 10, 20, or 30 lbs. As a result, you feel better, look better, and run better—a desirable trifecta for any runner. Plus, you gain a laundry list of health benefits that come with living at a healthy weight.

…and here's a bonus: you feel lighter on your feet. So while running there's never a moment you feel heavy or bogged down. Your movements become nimble. This makes running more pleasurable, and if leveraged, you will run faster.

Fat adapted running has the potential to melt fat away. It's the answer to the riddle of weight loss that stumps many runners. If you become a fat adapted runner your body will transform, period.

Recovery Speeds Up

A speedy recovery means quicker progressions, less burnout, and the prevention of injury. In other words, you reach more finish lines, and do so at a faster pace. What an incredible benefit for long-distance runners.

The fact is that a high-fat diet provides anti-inflammatory benefits. It also reduces pain, lowers your lactate load, and decreases oxidative stress. Add this up, and you recover faster and feel invincible while training. Now show up on race day and tell me how you feel.

Becoming a fat adapted runner will speed up recovery, and that's beneficial for any runner.

Save Money on Supplements

When you stop relying on sugar to run, there's less need for sugary supplements. No more pockets of gels or expensive sports drinks. It's just you, the road, and the fuel from within. Your dependency on external forms of energy significantly drops.

Sure, many fat adapted runners still use supplements, especially on race day. This helps you maintain a fast pace for longer. For example, many fat adapted professional runners still consume gels to remain on edge. But although supplements may still be required if speed is your goal, you won't need as many. Plus, you now have the option to cut supplements out entirely. That was my approach. I chose a cleaner, supplement-free path over a few extra seconds off my pace.

My goal isn't how fast I run during ultramarathons. It's about how good I feel. My focus is on well-being instead of speed, but that's just my goal. Your goal may be different. Either way, the point is you now have the option no matter what distance you run. Whether you run a 5k, half-marathon, marathon or ultramarathon, your supplement consumption will reduce.

Overall, fat adapted running will raise your fueling foundation. Even when you consume supplements on race day, if managed right, you won't hit the wall from a sugar depletion. You will eliminate "the wall," and marathon runners will be thankful for that.

Preparation Takes Less Time

Imagine waking up, drinking a glass of water, putting on your shoes, and running out the door…that's it. No more meal prepping. No more filling up bottles. No more stuffing your pockets with gels, and best of all, no more bulky running gear hanging off your body.

Can you imagine how simplistic running can be? Fat adapted running creates the chance at a minimalistic style of training. It helps simplify your running, so you have more energy to spare. Also, it releases some of the extra weight that long-distance running can create—that's right, no more extra baggage. Fat adapted running simplifies the process…and what a simple process running can be.

Stomach Issues Vanish

Ever experience stomach issues before, during, or after a run? I have, and trust me, we are not alone. The majority of runners experience stomach issues. Whether that be nausea, diarrheas, bloating, or stomach cramps. The fact is most runners suffer from gastrointestinal distress.

In the running world, gastrointestinal distress is better known as "GI Issues," and it's very real. As I mentioned in the introduction, fat adapted running was my cure for nausea. Who knew that a few tweaks in your diet could create such an incredible improvement? And you know what? A high-fat diet relieves your stomach in other ways too. Remember—there are numerous stomach issues that runners face. One of the most common is bloating on race day.

If you are not a fat adapted runner, you are sugar dependent. That's where the whole "carb-loading" method stems from. As you may know, many long-distance runners do some serious carb-loading building up to race day. In my opinion, that's why the percentage of runners who experience stomach issues is so high. This correlation is no coincidence. If you've ever loaded up on carbohydrates the night before a race, then you may be familiar with the feeling. The stomach distress basically becomes a part of the race day experience, but I'm here to tell you: stomach issues can vanish.

Bloating occurs with a disturbing increase in fiber consumption. Marathon runners know this uncomfortable stomach distress the best. Hitting the pizza buffet or spaghetti pot the night before a race can do more harm than good.

Now on race day, not only do you try to relieve bloating, but you run the risk of being stuck in the bathroom on race start. The porta potty is no place for a runner when the gun goes off. So remember—fewer carbs equals fewer stomach issues; however, your body must be accustomed to low carbs if you want to deviate from the carb-loading path.

Overall, fat adapted running works wonders on gut health. The further you run, the more you will appreciate this fact. So cut out the carbs, increase good fats, and watch your stomach issues disappear.

Gain More Freedom

If you like the freedom of running than you will love the extra freedom of fat adapted running. Imagine running extraordinary distances without the restraint of sugar consumption every few miles. No more relying on external fuel sources. The ball and chain are removed. Can you feel the freedom in that?

When I toed the starting line of my first 100-mile ultramarathon as a sugar-dependent runner, I had some concern. I knew my stomach eventually would reject gels, but I had no plan B. There was no telling how my body would respond, and just as I guessed…it didn't respond well.

The first 50 miles went well, but the second 50 miles was a brutal thrashing to the finish line. Both my mind and stomach were *screaming* to stop. Even so, regardless of how torturous the experience was, I pushed my way to the finish line.

Fast forward a few years later, and I toed the starting line of my first 200-mile ultramarathon, but this time, something different occurred. I felt confidence instead of worry. That's because I was fat adapted, not sugar dependent. Fat adapted running became a process to follow, and the outcome was the 200-mile finish line.

Now, as a runner who burns fat as fuel, there's little restriction on how far I can run. No fueling issues are holding me back. Before my first marathon, I feared "the wall." Now, I understand the wall is self-created through a disadvantaged diet. I now know that as long as I have fat in my body and faith in my soul, I can reach any distance of any length.

Today, there are no limitations in my running due to nutrition. My body can run as far as my mind will take it. As a fat adapted runner, you have access to a near-infinite supply of energy from within. Sure, running 200 miles wasn't easy, it was one of the toughest challenges of my life. I had blisters the size of water balloons, nosebleeds that flowed like rivers, and heat exhaustion that crippled my spirits, but as long as my nutrition was at a peak level, the possibilities were endless. All other issues could be managed as they arose. Yet, if you ask me, nutrition is the trickiest adversity we face as runners. Conquer nutrition, and there is a tremendous freedom in that.

So whether I'm running 10 miles, 20 miles, 30 miles, or even 40 miles, I do so with no food or water. I can run extraordinary distances without relying on external fuel sources. Can you feel the freedom in that? I sure can, and do you want to know the best part? This same freedom is available to anyone who is willing to take the right steps to transform their body, and that includes you! Are you ready to free yourself?

Health Improves Drastically

I won't get into the particular studies and research of how a high-fat diet can treat and reverse diseases. I didn't write this book to sell an idea. I wrote this book to provide a guide to become a fat adapted runner.

You see, I went through the hardships and came out the other side with a proven system. It's a system that can turn you into a fat burning machine. Although a high-fat diet will improve running, an improvement in health becomes a reciprocal of your efforts. In other words, *The Fat Adapted Running Formula*™ also improves your health. There are many diseases a high-fat diet has proven to help with.

Regarding symptoms, it's my understanding that a high-fat diet can help with low/high blood sugar, high blood triglycerides, high cholesterol, high blood pressure, heartburn, and migraines. That's only to name a few. Regarding disease, it's also my understanding that a high-fat diet can help with cardiovascular disease, obesity, diabetes, fatty liver disease, bipolar, Parkinson's, and epilepsy. Again, that's only to name a few of the many benefits.

By morphing your body back to the way it's designed to function, you work towards eliminating the many lifestyle diseases we collectively face today. A lifestyle disease extends from an unhealthy lifestyle, and an unhealthy lifestyle extends from poor eating habits and a lack of exercise. So, generally speaking, all that's required to reverse a lifestyle disease is to live a healthier lifestyle. You must eat healthily and be active. What could be better than fat adapted running?

Note: storing fat is a function of the body and is a product of our evolution. Our ancestors were hunter-gathers. It was feast or famine. Our bodies store fat to keep us alive. So when it comes to our survival, storing fat is actually a wonderful thing. Without the ability to store fat, who knows if a human being could have survived this long. Let's save the evolutionary biology for another time. Today, let's learn how to become a fat adapted runner.

Over time we've become less efficient at burning fat, and more dependent on sugar. The problem is that carbohydrates (sugars) break down, and store as fat if not used for energy…and the fat stays there. As you can see, we've made it very difficult for our bodies to efficiently burn fat and very easy to gain weight.

Fat adapted running may not just be the answer to our running prayers, but it may be our savior to well-being. It morphs and throws our bodies back in time before the sugar explosion of a diet we've become so accustomed to. It brings us back to a normal human metabolism.

Sugar Cravings Disintegrate

In the next chapter, I'll explain why sugar cravings set our body up for disaster. The problem is how sugar digests quickly, becomes addictive, and converts to fat if not utilized. Basically, sugar cravings make us become more sugar dependent and cause us to gain weight.

Being addicted to sugar is not much different from being addicted to drugs. In fact, some studies show sugar is even more addictive than cocaine. Here's what I can tell you from experience: once your body turns fat adapted, sugar cravings fade away. Instead of requiring self-discipline not to eat that piece of cake, you just don't want it. Food that at one time tasted delicious begins to taste fake. It may hurt your stomach from even trying a little piece. You may also begin associating sugary processed food as something closer to a poison than a meal. The term "food" begins to have a new meaning.

Sure, not every sugary piece of processed food is going to taste bad, but the more fat adapted you become, and the more natural you eat, the more artificial this food tastes. Soon you don't even want that soda or donut. In other words, you no longer need self-discipline, you just need to be fat adapted.

Overall, fewer sugar cravings help you become a fat adapted runner faster, and the quicker you become fat adapted, the sooner you will run further. Wouldn't you like to run that marathon or ultramarathon in the near future? You can reach it through fat adaptation within your body and the determination within your heart.

Sustainable Energy Moves You Forward

No matter how much you love to run, there will be days you don't feel like running. Even with all the motivation in the world, on some days, exhaustion will try to overcome your drive. As an experienced long-distance runner, I'm here to tell you those are the days to capitalize on. Those are the days designed for improvement. Those are the days for growth. Pushing through mental resistance in your training is how you develop positive habits. Develop enough of them, and you won't need to push through your training program. Training runs will merely become a behavior dictated by your subconscious. You will begin to feel pulled through your training. It will be a natural occurrence.

So how does combating hesitation in your training relate to fat adapted running? Well, when you are fat adapted, you develop a dominant form of sustainable energy. No more playing victim to sugar highs and crashes. There are no more roller coaster rides of energy—you now have a balanced abundant stream.

Now try going on that run after a long day. Rarely will you reach a depletion of energy so low that you skip a training day. Rarely will you surrender the day to the couch due to exhaustion. Those moments of hesitation before a training run disappear into thin air, but there's no abracadabra. It's not magic, it's fat adaptation. No hocus-pocus. It's an efficient fat adapted metabolism and the balanced energy that comes with it. So even when you're tired, with sustainable energy, you won't reach a breaking point. You will have enough energy to complete your training run and move along steadily to race day.

Before fat adapted running, I became exhausted early in the night. Sure, I'm what you would call a "morning person" and I still go to bed relatively early; however, before I became a fat adapted runner, there were nights I'd fall asleep incredibly early. Forget about a date to the movie theatre with my wife. It didn't matter if buildings crashed or explosions rumbled the walls of the theatre, when the lights dimmed, it was shut-eye. No, not even when my wife smacked me in the head would I stay up during a night at the movies. Date night became less of a night with popcorn and laughs and more of a night with closed eyes and snoring. Falling to bed early not only affected my social life, but it made fitting in a training run more difficult as well. Becoming exhausted was out of my control. Or so I thought…

You see, everything changed when I incorporated a high-fat diet with my long-distance running. It was mesmerizing. I learned falling asleep early was due to the way I eat. My early nights of shut-eye wasn't due to my biorhythm, it was due to my sugar addiction. Sugar crashes dominated my life, and fat adapted running changed it all.

Once I achieved a level of pure and healthy sustainable energy, I entered the driver's seat. Today, when I'm ready to go to bed, I acknowledge it and close my eyes. Or if I choose to stay awake, then I remain awake. Falling asleep is just as easy because I am not a victim of sugar highs. With sustainable energy created by a high-fat diet, when you are tired you close your eyes, and sleep comes easily.

Fat adapted running will provide boundless energy. But remember, there are both good fats and bad fats. Not all fats are created equal. We will touch on this subject in a later chapter. For now, understand that once you become a fat adapted runner, food no longer becomes a source of energy. Food is now a tool to .ignite the energy from within. What a miracle fat adapted running can be.

Focus Becomes Laser Sharp

When I began my fat adapted running journey, do you know what I noticed first? Here's a hint: it wasn't an improvement in running, and it wasn't how fast my sugar craving dissolved. What I noticed first was my laser-sharp focus. It was completely unexpected. One day I was reading a document and BAM…it hit me. The brain fog lifted, and my focus dialed itself inwards. I could pay attention longer, my mind didn't drift as much, and I even felt a physical sensation in my head. After some research, I noticed this was a common phenomenon of a high-fat diet. So here's the best news of all: this laser-sharp focus that was available to me is also available to you. It just takes a few small adjustments to your eating habits.

My improvement in brain function didn't occur coincidentally. The change was apparent. It was crystal clear, and I'm not alone.

Research shows that a high-fat diet improves brain function, memory, learning, and clarity of thought. Basically, the fog lifts and your focus sharpens. The changes are jaw dropping and it usually takes just a few weeks to kick in.

Don't forget, making a drastic shift in your eating habits can first cause more harm than good. That's because your body can go through withdrawal from the reduction of sugar. So don't let a small step backward prevent you from a gigantic leap forward.

The Hidden Benefit

Overall, fat adapted running will not only improve your running, it will improve your life. Your performance enhances in every aspect, and the best benefit is its hidden benefit.

What's the hidden benefit of fat adapted running? The answer: *longevity*. Running with a high-fat diet will bring longevity to your running. That's because it takes training and racing from an acidic and corrosive form of movement to one of balance and harmony. The type of balance that can last a lifetime.

So whether you want to make running easier, lose weight, speed up recovery, ditch the supplements, improve gut health, reduce time preparing, feel free, become healthier, eliminate sugar cravings, develop sustainable energy, or improve brain function, fat adaptation will take you there. You just have to put in the effort. It will take hard work up front, but the investment will pay dividends in the long run.

So…what's next? Where do you go from here? Well, becoming a fat adapted runner of course. So before we jump outside to run, we must first stop by the kitchen and build a solid foundation on fat adapted running nutrition. Remember the food pyramid you learned in grade school? Prepare to wipe that from your psyche. Throw it out the window. It won't serve you as fat adapted runner. So prepare yourself as I walk you through building a solid foundation for fat adapted running. Because I know this for sure: no one wants to build a house on a shaky foundation. Ready to build your fat adapted skyscraper? If so, read on as we jump into *The Foundation.*

CHAPTER 3:

The Foundation

What creates extraordinary energy? This seemingly challenging question can appear complicated at first, but the fact is, it's not. With the right strategy and effort, developing the energy required to achieve your fat adapted running goals becomes a simple process.

Whether you're running your first mile, marathon, or ultramarathon, the true measure of success is not in crossing the finish line. The real success is making an everlasting change that is sustainable for a lifetime, no matter the circumstances. The start to your fat adapted running journey begins with building an unbreakable foundation.

Did you know that if all the muscles in the human body worked together and pulled in one direction, it would equal 25 tons of pulling power? That's equivalent to pulling more than three fully-grown elephants at once! So next time you feel like you don't have the energy to run, guess what? You do.

Even with the vast amount of potential energy within the human body, we still face a big problem as runners. When we run, we tend to focus on external ways of creating energy instead of creating energy from within. We look for the next sports drink or gel loaded with quick hits of sugar, run until near empty, and then take another hit. Although this does provide us with a jolt of energy to keep running, it's only a short-term fix.

If you wish to tap into your internal energy and become fat adapted, it will take a commitment to a natural lifestyle. What I learned was the more natural I ate, the easier and quicker fat adapted running became. Here's the secret to developing the foundation for fat adapted running: EAT NATURAL.

I've made the transition through my own running journey. I went from running marathons while popping gels and guzzling sports drinks to routinely running 31 miles (50k) with no food or water. Today, I live a more holistic lifestyle and run 100-mile ultramarathons by primarily burning my stored fat as fuel.

Here's an important point, I'm not special, I'm not a gifted athlete; however, I do push myself, I educate myself, and most importantly, I built a solid foundation and with that, fat adapted running became possible. Look, I have good runs and bad runs like anyone else. The only difference is that I've taken advantage of the way my body functions and anyone can do the same—so can you.

I can't promise building a fat adapted foundation happens overnight. What I will promise is that it has created everlasting energy and weight loss in my own life. I've run 100 miles weighing 200lbs and I've run the same distance at 175lbs. The difference has been in how I eat, not in how many miles I've run, and as an ultramarathon runner, you sure run a whole lot of miles!

So what's the fat adapted running foundation all about? Well, it's the starting point to the shift in your energy. The following information will help transform your body into one that can become fat adapted. In other words, once you build your foundation, fat adapted running will become easier.

There are no guarantees in life, but here is my promise to you: once you start feeling good—and I mean like *really* good—you won't ever go back.

Remember: it's not a diet change, but a lifestyle change that's necessary. Change the way you eat and change your life forever!

So here is the million-dollar question: How do you build your fat adapted running foundation and transform into a fit and lean runner who burns fat primarily as fuel? Well, you first have to understand the difference between *fitness* and *health*.

Fitness vs. Health

Most people do not truly understand the difference between fitness and health. Sometimes you must sit down and really consider the contrast before you grasp a real understanding. Simply put, fitness is the ability to perform athletic activity, whereas health is the state in which all the systems in your body are working at their best.

Here's the secret: don't just run to become *fit*, run to become both *fit* and *healthy*. This is something all the greatest athletes know instinctively.

So now the question shifts. The question now becomes this: How do you build your fat adapted running foundation and reach a peak fit and healthy state, while increasing your endurance and speed in the process? Well, it all starts with a healthy lifestyle…

Health, Fitness, and Running

First, understand that whatever you put into your body is exactly what you get out. So if you put in a sticky bun, then guess what? You feel like a sticky bun. On the other hand, if you put in a supercharged, alkalized, power-veggie shake, then, BAM…that's how you feel! Your body does not have the ability to turn poor nutritional choices into ones of high quality. Our cells, muscles, skin, and bones are built by the food that we supply it. We literally are what we eat.

The first time I ran 100 miles was brutal. I muscled my way to the finish line with nothing more than the clothes on my back and the drive in my heart. The first 50 miles went okay, but during the second 50 miles I was just trying not to throw up. Yes, it's complicated to rationalize an irrational act like running 24 hours half-naked through the woods, with an intense focus on preventing yourself from throwing up on your shoes. Many runners quit that day, but I was fortunate enough to complete the race. When I reached the finish line, I noticed something interesting. I noticed some athletes appeared to be in good shape. Their post-race condition immediately got me thinking, "There must be a better way."

So I began to read. Remember, knowledge alone is not power; rather, knowledge with action is power. When you read something and then apply it, that's when you better your running, and your life. I began to teach myself about nutrition. I tried many different approaches and suddenly it all came together. Eventually, I realized that eating all-natural is the way a human being was born to eat. Since fat adaptation is our normal metabolic state, eating real food is the quickest path to becoming a fat adapted runner, it's the foundation to fat adapted running. With that said, I will share tips and tricks to help strengthen your fat adapted running foundation, but first, start by eating *real* food.

Eat Real Food

The key to building your fat adapted foundation is to eat real food. Stop eating food by-products and eat real *live* food. Get rid of junk like bread, pasta, cake, bars, and soda. For example, eat salads instead of sandwiches, vegetable soup instead of macaroni, and almonds or avocados instead of breakfast bars.

By eating all natural, you allow your body to digest and metabolize the right way. Soon you will begin primarily burning the fat already stored in your body for energy. This would be instead of fueling with refined sugars through processed foods. Also, once you start to eat all natural, the body detoxifies itself from all the harmful pollutants in processed foods. Remember this: processed foods are toxic to the body. So if you're consuming more waste from toxins than you're eliminating, your body will never burn fat, but by eating real live foods, you will naturally burn fat and use internal energy all day.

By eating all natural foods like vegetables and nuts you also reduce sugar cravings, which cause you to overeat. So now you will begin to eat more good fats, which are the key to becoming a fat adapted runner who can run long distances.

The Industry Standard

If you eat an average American diet, then your biggest threat right now is refined carbs and sugars. Refined carbs are foods like bread, pasta, pastries, breakfast bars, and soda.

The problem with this type of food is your body digests them quickly. They enter into your bloodstream as sugar. Some are used for energy, but the majority are stored as body fat. Then your blood sugar drops and because refined sugar is so addictive, your body doesn't just want more, it needs more. You go through withdrawal and become hungry again. So you eat more, digest quick, gain more fat, and the cycle continues until you become overweight and suffer from disease.

Eat Refined Sugar/Carbs to *Digest Quick* → *Left Over Energy Stored As Fat* → *Blood Sugar Drops* → *Withdraw + Hunger* → *Eat More!*

One big problem is how companies add sugar and sweeteners in nearly everything. It's in your milk, your juice, your pasta, and even in your salad dressing—you name it. If the ingredients do not say *"sugar"* then it's being disguised with names such as *"high fructose corn syrup"* or *"aspartame"* or "dextrose," but they all have the same sugary addictive effects. Perhaps they add excess sugar to make the food taste better. Or, perhaps it's because if you're addicted to their product then you will buy more of it. Regardless, it's supply and demand, so if we as consumers demand it, then the food industry will supply it.

Sugar is an addictive drug that has shown to cause diabetes, obesity, stomach problems, and disease. Too much sugar will destroy your chances at becoming a fat adapted runner. As you feed your body more sugar, it will become dependent on sugar for energy, not fat. In particular, what's the most common source of sugar in our diets today? The answer: *soft drinks*. Tens of millions of cold beverages are consumed daily in the US alone. Whatever is not used as energy is quickly stored as fat in your body. That's including your soda, diet soda, juices, and teas. Here's the problem, if your body is continually burning sugar as fuel, it will become dependent on it. Soon your body burns sugar for energy much easier than fat. Now it becomes rather difficult to tap into your stored body fat for fuel.

That's why you must primarily eat good fats and vegetables when building your foundation for fat adapted running. By doing so, you will teach your body to burn fat as fuel while providing it the right nutrients, instead of relying solely on sugar as fuel. Vegetables and good fats make us feel fuller for longer without the sugar cravings. Without sugar to burn, your body will default to fat. Eventually, it prefers good fat to burn and that's when you have constructed a solid fat adapted foundation.

So make your goal to eat natural and healthy and you'll naturally become lean, you'll naturally become healthy, and you'll naturally start to burn fat as fuel.

If you want your body to burn fat as fuel efficiently, you must morph it into an efficient machine. You can't ride around town in an old gas-guzzling SUV, expecting to burn fuel like a new hybrid. You will need a new engine. Fortunately, your body doesn't require a part swap to become more efficient at burning fat; however, it will need a shift in focus to develop new healthy habits.

So, continue reading as I provide the building blocks to your fat adapted running foundation. Between eating right, developing more energy, and detoxification, you will be well on your way to becoming a fat adapted runner.

Drink More Water

We are our cells. There are a trillion cells within our body that make up who we are. How do cells live? Yes, you guessed it: *water.* Our bodies are made up of more than 68% water. This statistic alone should prove how vital water is for us. If cells provide us with life and energy and they need water to survive, doesn't it make sense to drink more water?

Also, experts say that drinking water suppresses appetite and curbs cravings. This will help with the sugar withdrawal through the fat adaptation process. Plus, increasing your water intake helps you metabolize fat quicker. Drinking more water improves your body function, helping it reach its normal metabolic state—one that burns fat primarily as fuel. As you can see, drinking more water will strengthen your foundation as you get ready to embark on your fat adapted running journey.

Eat High Water Content Foods

In addition to drinking more water, a large portion of your daily diet should be in high water content foods like green vegetables. This helps the body cleanse itself instead of clog it. Don't forget, if you're bringing in more waste from toxins than what your body can get rid of, then you will never burn fat. So by cleansing your body with water-enriched foods, you build a solid foundation for fat adaptation to take place.

What type of food is water enriched? Here's a list of the most common:

- Lettuce
- Asparagus
- Broccoli
- Beets
- Celery
- Cucumbers
- Green beans
- Kale

- Parsley
- Spinach
- Squash
- Zucchini

Before you stick a piece of food in your mouth, consider if it will allow your metabolic river to flow, or stick a dam into it. Remember this: a portion of your hydration should come from food. So on top of drinking plenty of water, be sure to eat plenty of high water content food.

Eat Good Fats

First, understand that we as human beings are designed to store fat. This is how our bodies have adapted through time. It's a survival instinct. So if our bodies are designed to store fat, how do we tap into it for fuel? Easy, we turn our bodies into fat burning machines. We teach it to burn fat efficiently.

Let's go back to the coal-burning example from a previous chapter. Burning sugar for fuel is like lighter fluid. You ignite it with a flame, there's a big flash, then POOF…it's gone. Burning sugar is the same way: you eat it, it's used for immediate energy, then POOF…you're on empty. After the POOF is where many runners "hit the wall."

On the other hand, burning fat as fuel is like a coal fire. You ignite it with a flame, then slow and steady, it burns through the night. Burning fat is the same way. Fat stores in your body and burns at a slow and steady pace. When your body burns fat as fuel, you tap into a nearly infinite supply of energy that leads to a nearly endless amount of possibilities in your running.

The problem is our society holds fat as the culprit for weight gain. So companies promote their nonfat options like non-fat cookies, cakes, crackers, chips, etc. We then consume these non-fat alternatives thinking it's healthy because there's no fat—this couldn't be any further from the truth. Completely eliminating fat from your diet is one of the worst things you can do. Essential fatty acids are needed in every cell of your body to function, especially your brain...and of course, they are necessary to become a fat adapted runner.

However, not all fats are created equal. There are good fats and bad fats. Here are a few recommendations to get you started:

- Avocados
- Almonds
- Hazelnuts
- Macadamias
- Pumpkin seeds
- Olive oil
- Flaxseed oil

You can also take an essential oil every day. I will discuss essential oils in the next chapter. Now don't forget, more good fats equals fewer sugar cravings, which helps you become fat adapted.

Alkalize Your Body

We all know on a basic level that some foods are better for us and some foods are worse. Yet where does "*unhealthy*" actually end and where does "*healthy*" begin? Where is the line drawn between a hotdog and a cucumber?

One way to determine what's healthy and what's not is viewing the concept from an alkaline vs. acidic point of view. Our bodies need to maintain a slightly higher alkaline environment to function properly, and this is monitored through our pH levels. Our trillions of cells also rely on an alkaline environment to prevent cellular damage.

Disease flourishes in an acidic environment. So to prevent acidic conditions like fatigue, stress, and obesity, we need to maintain a healthy pH balance. These types of energy-draining conditions prevent us from improving as runners and becoming a healthier person who can transform into a fat adapted runner. So when people become overweight...guess what? It's not usually a fat problem but an acidic problem. Too much acid in your body produces more insulin, thus storing more fat. Plus, you become inefficient at burning stored fat. Most people become overweight because although they are storing fat, their bodies have a hard time tapping into it. It's like a one-way valve. Fat is entering in but not out. The key is to transform your body into a fat burning machine and it starts by alkalizing it.

How do you alkalize your body? Simple: go green, go green, go green! The majority of your daily diet should consist of alkalizing foods such as green vegetables, raw almonds, avocados, and lemon. Furthermore, you want to avoid acidic-forming foods like certain kinds of animal meat, dairy products, white refined foods, sugar, etc. You can also alkalize your body through a green superfood alkalizing powder or by simply adding lemon to your water.

When your body rids itself of its acidic environment, it can metabolize more efficiently. An efficient metabolism is a start to naturally develop energy and to burn fat. So alkalize your body and become lighter on your feet, healthier in your body, and more energized than you've ever felt in your life. From here, you can build your foundation for fat adapted running.

Always Maximize Nutrition

When building your fat adapted foundation, it's essential to understand nutrition and maximize it as much as possible. Remember, proper nutrition will make your body more efficient at burning fat. So first, if you don't know already, the seven components of food are carbohydrates, proteins, fats, vitamins, minerals, water, and fiber. If it's been a while, be sure to freshen up on the basics of each.

There's no secret to nutrition; it's a process. Nutrition is providing what your body needs to function properly. Here are a few tips to help in the process:

- Drink water before or after meals, not during.
- Choose filtered water over tap water and add lemon.
- Combine foods properly; for example, eat fruit only on an empty stomach.
- Watch your sugar; eat fewer fruits and more vegetables.
- Fruit is a treat; consider it your new natural lifestyle candy.
- Eat relaxed; if you're in a rush, you will overeat.
- Eat organic; this avoids pesticides, growth hormones, and antibiotics.
- Don't count calories, just eat clean.
- Start each day with essential oils.
- Seasonings turn your meal into superfood.
- Pay attention to the ingredients in the dressing and dips you use.
- Wheatgrass is a powerful choice for nutrient delivery.
- Add nuts like almonds and pistachios to salads.
- Add vegetables to take-out salads, remove croutons, and use oily dressing.
- Always remove bread from quick take-out meals like sandwiches.
- If you eat meat or eggs, they should be organic and pasteurized when possible.

Each small tip applied to your daily routine will add up to one giant positive change in your body. Understand that healthy improvements don't add up, they compound. Each day you are building from a healthier you. Make a few small changes each week and listen to your body. Each incremental step is one more building block to the construction of your fat adapted running foundation.

Ditch the Food Pyramid

The key to a healthy diet is to drink elephant's milk. Yes, 10-12 servings of elephants milk per day keeps the doctor away. Okay, this may sound a bit odd to some. But if you ask me, so does drinking cow's milk. Cows don't even drink cow's milk, so why would we?

In any case, through history, not only did cow's milk make it to our lips, it also chiseled a spot right smack in the middle of our food pyramid. This same food pyramid that has been heavily influenced by the agriculture industry tells us what daily servings we need to achieve optimum nourishment in our lives.

Personally, on my nutritional journey, I haven't sipped milk in over ten years. Stop drinking milk and watch how healthy you may begin to feel. Milk has been proven to have many adverse side effects like mucus production, allergies, irritable bowel syndrome, malabsorption of nutrients, obesity, and mineral and amino deficiencies.

An ideal food regimen is 70% live foods (mainly vegetables and some fruits), 10% plant-based proteins or fish, 10% carbohydrates, and 10% quality oil. Sure, you can use the standard food pyramid and you still may become fat adapted. Yet, to assure your success, I recommend following as close to these percentages as possible.

Look, I'm not saying you have to stop eating carbohydrates or jump on some strict ketogenic diet to become fat adapted. What I'm saying is to be conscious of what you consume, eat live food, and keep your sugar intake to a minimal. The more drive you have to become fat adapted, the more eating habits you will be willing to change.

Breath Through the Abdominal

As you become fat adapted you will feel sluggish and tired at first. So it's critical to try and develop energy any way possible. That's where breathing comes in. Here's the thing: breathing provides oxygen to your moving muscles, thus creating more energy for your runs. The more you focus on your breathing, the more energy you can create. Plus, it's my understanding that breathing exercises improve the function of your metabolism and aid in digestion. When you breathe deeply, it increases your oxygen supply; this, in turn, promotes fat burning. The key is to breathe correctly.

Try this: take a deep breath. Go ahead…one deep breath…notice anything?

Did you breathe directly from your chest? This is a shallow way of breathing. When you breathe from the chest, you are only using part of your lung capacity. To take advantage of your lungs' full capacity, it's critical to breathe from the diaphragm, focusing on your abdominal.

You can also take power breaths periodically throughout the day. A 2-4-1 ratio works well. For example, inhale for 10 seconds, hold for 20 seconds and exhale for 5 seconds. Not only does this increase energy, but it reduces anxiety, relaxes the body, relieves stress, and strengthens the immune system.

Find what works best for you, then make sure you focus on your breathing while running. Deep breathing through meditation before or after your run can work wonders as well. So, breathe through the abdominal to increase energy and construct a solid foundation for fat adapted running.

Build With Aerobic Activity

To become a better runner, along with excellent nutrition, you must be physically active. This is done in two ways, through *aerobic* activity and *anaerobic* activity.

First there is *aerobic* activity. Aerobic literally means *"with oxygen."* It's when you exercise at a moderate pace like during your long runs. When you perform aerobic activity, you are mainly burning fat as fuel, your breathing isn't too heavy, and you can still hold a conversation. When you run long distance, you are actually building your aerobic base. This type of exercise strengthens your heart, lungs, blood vessels, and all other aerobic muscles. It helps build your fat adapted running foundation. Consider aerobic activity like the foundation of a house. If you build a house on a shaky foundation, the house, meaning your body, will collapse. You will feel tired, achy, and possibly injure yourself. Whereas if you have a solid and sturdy foundation you can build a skyscraper. You will have the potential to run harder for longer, ultimately becoming more enduring.

So now that you have your super-sturdy aerobic foundation, let's talk about *anaerobic* activity, meaning *"without oxygen."* Anaerobic activity refers to exercise at a fast pace. It's your short bursts of power, like when you run a sprint or lift heavy weights. Anaerobic activity is when you get out of breath and burn sugar primarily as fuel. It's what gives you power! It's what gives you speed! It's what gives you the ability to develop tunnel vision straight to the finish line!

There's a place for *anaerobic* activity. I will discuss increasing speed in a future chapter. Simply stated, *aerobic* activity is what truly builds your fat adapted foundation. Slow and steady training will promote a fat adapted body, so in the beginning, keep your pace slow.

Move Throughout Your Day

Movement creates more movement. The more you move throughout your day, the more momentum you develop. So when it's time for a run, guess what? You are already energized and ready to go. Momentum becomes incredibly helpful at the beginning of *The Fat Adapted Running Formula™*, where your body feels heavy fatigue.

So how do you gain momentum for your runs? Easy, prime the pump—meaning: build up momentum through your day. Do things like standing up and working, take the stairs instead of the elevator, and go for walks.

Do you know how I get the best parking spot at the mall every time I visit? I don't look for the closest parking spot at the store, I look for the farthest and walk. Every small increase in movement adds up and compounds to more energy and a body that can burn fat more efficiently. Plus, constant movement throughout the day is aerobic activity and remember, during aerobic exercise, you primarily burn fat as fuel.

Without realizing it, you are strengthening your fat metabolism throughout your day. So, move slow and steady and keep moving forward.

Things to Not Do

So now that you know what to do…here's a few things to not do, things you can reduce or eliminate, starting today. By avoiding these as much as possible, you will prevent hurting your progress to fat adapted running, especially in the beginning as you build your foundation. These recommendations are solely based on my personal experience. Some I never consumed in the first place. I reduced or eliminated the following:

- Refined Sugar/carbs
- Processed fats
- Meat
- Dairy products
- Alcohol
- Nicotine
- Drugs

Basically, everything you will find at your next barbecue. These can be viewed as acidic addictions that have the potential to destroy your insides. If your body is too busy fighting off the symptoms of acidic additions, then how much energy will it have for running? The answer: not much. No one is perfect; I'm sure not, but here's what I can tell you. It's a fight uphill at first, but once you reach the tipping point, it becomes a more stable slope to greater health and a fat adapted lifestyle.

Again, here's my promise: once you start to feel good, I mean *really* good, you won't want the bad stuff. Don't make this a diet—because it's not. The weight loss industry is worth billions of dollars; we are programmed to believe we should "go on" a diet. Yet the concept of "going on" a diet doesn't actually exist. It's either you eat real food and primarily burn fat as fuel, or you're not actually eating food at all. So the key is *not* to "go on a diet," the key is to eat when you're hungry and to eat real food.

Here's What to Do Next...

Building your foundation is not about perfection. Eating clean and natural as a lifestyle will require some zigging and zagging. Don't hold yourself to an all-or-nothing standard. It's about making healthier choices each day and not "dieting," but eating the way a human is designed to eat—that is, eating *real* food.

Follow *The Foundation* and you will become fat adapted. This chapter alone will transform your body into a fat burning machine; however, if you want to become a fat adapted *runner* who can run longer distances by burning fat as fuel, then let's move onto the next chapter: *The Bridge*. In this chapter, you'll fine-tune your nutritional efforts and make the changes necessary to transfer from a mere fat adapted *person*, to a fat adapted *runner*. So continue reading to achieve maximum results in your fat adapted running journey.

CHAPTER 4:

The Bridge

Now that you've established your foundation, it's time to construct your bridge. This chapter of *The Fat Adapted Running Formula*™ is called *The Bridge* because it bridges the gap between someone who burns fat efficiently for everyday life to someone who burns it enough to become a fat adapted runner.

The Bridge is about fine-tuning your fat metabolism. It's about transforming your body so it can burn fat as fuel while running long distances. Some of my methodologies may seem extreme, but it takes a radical action to make a radical change in your body.

Remember—becoming fat adapted doesn't happen overnight. It takes a continuous effort and a constant awareness of your eating habits; however, if you stick with it, eventually you'll reach the tipping point. Instead of living on a slippery slope back to sugary substances and processed foods, one day…the scale tips. Now it feels like a more stable slope in a healthier direction. It begins to feel natural to eliminate foods and behaviors that don't serve your fat-burning metabolism.

I can tell you from experience. Once I reached the other side, ultramarathons went from a torturous build-up and release process to an incredible journey of struggle and growth. Here's the best part of all: I now know I have found longevity in my running. I now know I can run ultramarathon distances into the late stages of my life if I desire. I know this as I've taught my body to fuel naturally from the inside, instead of an acidic, artificial way from the outside.

The following tips of *The Bridge* incorporate what you've learned from *The Foundation* and fine-tune them even more. In this chapter, it's critical to listen to your body. Listen close and soon enough your body will fall into alignment. The way you eat and how you run will just feel…right.

Looking back to when I first started, I wish I'd stumbled upon a book like this one. A written formula from someone who has pushed the envelope of human endurance as a fat adapted runner. It would have taken much less time to get to where I'm at today. So here's my gift to you: Time! *The Bridge* is about saving time by achieving *the greatest maximum results in the shortest period of time.* So continue reading for the most effective nutritional steps to catapult you from a fat adapted person to a fat adapted runner.

Cut Out Grain Completely

When I first started fat adapted running, I wanted to find a few big dominos up front. You know, one or two steps I could initially apply that would have the most significant impact. Through trial and error, I found what nutritional changes produce the *greatest maximum results in the shortest period of time.*

Going grain-free was the first step I took towards becoming a fat adapted runner and was by far one of the most effective. In my mind, since carbohydrates break down into sugars, this was an obvious decision to follow. Although I'd already eliminated bread and pasta, this meant no more granola, oats, brown rice, rye, buckwheat and yes…even quinoa.

I understand this may be tough for some and it's not required in fat adapted running. As long as you keep your carbohydrate intake to a minimum and be sure when you eat grains they are low-starch, you'll be fine; however, I recommend cutting grains out completely.

If you're still unsure about cutting out all grains, then I suggest you listen to your body. When I listened to mine, I noticed it responded much better by eliminating grains entirely. As I stated, eliminating bread and pasta make a huge difference and was a great starting point. It's easy to remove the bread from sandwiches, eat lettuce wraps, toss the crouton from salad or order a side of vegetables instead of pasta. Most grain products are processed anyway. So when you eliminate all processed foods from your diet, as recommended in *The Foundation*, your fat adapted running will rapidly improve.

Please note: eliminating all processed foods is not required in fat adapted running…but it certainly speeds up the process and you feel great! By eliminating grains and processed foods, you will reduce your sugar intake significantly. A reduction in sugar helps your body find a new way to fuel itself…and that's where fat comes in.

Discover the Magic of Essential Oils

One of the most impactful steps you can take to speed up the process of fat adaptation is taking an essential oil. The use of essential oils dates back over five thousand years ago. Not only are oils one of the best tools for becoming fat adapted, they are one of the best forms of medicine on the planet.

Here's the thing: taking an essential oil isn't some miracle solution or magical pill to burn fat as fuel. Nothing can be more beneficial than eating a healthy diet rich in green water-soluble vegetables and good fats; however, it helps…and in a big way.

For example, essential oils can speed up your metabolism, help with digestion, and naturally boost your energy. You basically become fat adapted quicker. Plus, if you take some before meals, you will significantly reduce sugar cravings. I can tell you this from experience. By consuming less sugar you will speed up the transformation of becoming a fat adapted runner.

My preferred type and the one I always recommend is flaxseed oil. After my morning glass of water, it's the first thing I put in my body every day. I'm not recommending taking essential oils as the only way, this is just what I do, and it's helped me along my journey into fat adapted running.

Practice Intermediate Fasting

Have you ever thought about what the word breakfast means? Here, look at the word: *breakfast*.

Okay, now look at it one more time: *break-fast*.

Yes, two words: *break* and *fast*. Breakfast literally means *"breaking the fast."* That's because it's the first meal of your day. It's the first meal after a long sleep with no food or water.

Intermediate fasting works wonders in accelerating the transformation process into fat adapted running. No, it's not the only way, but again, it's a dietary habit that will expedite the process into becoming a fat adapted runner.

Despite common beliefs, humans don't need to eat every single day. Technically, humans can go for multiple days without eating. That's why we store body fat. Plus, fasting on a regular basis becomes easier as you become more efficient at burning fat. That's versus when the body is dependent on sugar as its primary fuel source and feels hungry every few hours.

Intermediate fasting was and still is a daily practice of mine. Some days I go until 7:00 pm without eating anything and other days, just a few hours. Most mornings I have a few tablespoons of flaxseed oil and sometimes a cup of coffee or tea with no sugar and then fast until the evening. Remember—milk and creamers are typically filled with sugar. I've found that organic liquid stevia which can be bought from a natural food store is an excellent alternative. It's also a useful tool to wean yourself off the sugar in your coffee or tea.

So, why add in the coffee or tea with essential oils anyway? Well, for many reasons. First, the caffeine is a natural stimulant. Not only does it improve mental clarity and concentration, it also suppresses your appetite. As you can imagine, this makes fasting easier.

Then add in the essential oil, assuming you're not eating anything that raises your blood sugar, and your body will start to prefer burning fat. Soon your body even begins to burn fat while you sleep and continues the process upon awakening. This becomes possible if you keep your good fat intake high and your sugar intake low.

Monday is the perfect day to fast since you are more likely to indulge over the weekend. Also, if fasting becomes difficult through the day, eat a few handfuls of nuts to curb your appetite.

It doesn't matter to your body whether you just ate fat or it comes from your fat stores. Your body will continue to burn fat until insulin levels spike from sugar intake. Moral of the story: practice intermediate fasting to become a fat adapted runner. Start your morning with good fats and add caffeine to make fasting easier.

Use Fuel Low in Sugar

As you now know, I eat and fuel all natural—no performance supplements such as powders, gels, or sports drinks. So, naturally, my sugars are low when running. Yes, your body needs sugar when you run; however, it becomes a balancing act during a race of too little or too much.

How you fuel during a run is a reflection of how you eat outside of running. For example, if you eat processed foods and sugary beverages, then you probably need more gels and sports drinks when running. Conversely, if you are an efficient fat burning machine, you can fuel long races with low-sugar foods and keep your energy balanced.

It's funny; when I'm out, and people see I don't drink alcohol or eat desserts or bread, they think it's a struggle. I have to admit, at first it was. Even to this day, I still have a few psychological snacking barriers I need to forgo; however, what most people don't understand is that it's not a struggle anymore because the long-term superpower of fat adapted running completely outweighs the short-term sugar fix.

By keeping sugars low, you can run with sustainable energy that balances your running. Here is where you will avoid crashes on race day that are due to excess sugars. So, if you are as passionate about long-distance running as I am, specifically ultrarunning for me, there is no decision to make. Sugar indulgence is not worth its consequences.

Now don't get me wrong, my eating habits aren't flawless. I just make healthy decisions the majority of the time. Also, keep your post-run alcohol consumption to a minimal. I eventually cut out alcohol entirely because it hurt my progress. Eventually—and ironically enough—the cleaner I ate, the more my body rejected alcohol anyway.

If you do cut out your favorite food or drinks to keep your sugars low, replace it with a minimal amount of fruit to satisfy your sugar cravings. Eat fruit on an empty stomach so your body can quickly digest it. For example, after dinner, if you usually drink a milkshake, eat your favorite fruit instead.

Here's What to Do Next...

Follow the information outlined in *The Bridge* and you will achieve *the greatest maximum results in the shortest period of time*. In other words, you will become fat adapted quicker. Next, move onto *The Transformation,* where you take your fat adapted running body and actually start running. In this chapter, you will receive a set of training programs for every distance to progressively morph into a fat burning machine. Let's continue reading and start running.

CHAPTER 5:

The Transformation

A re you ready to begin running? *The Transformation* is where theory becomes fact. Here is where you take advantage of your newfound fat adapted running body and start burning fat as fuel while you run.

Ready to get started? Okay, listen up, I really want you to lean into this one. Next to removing grains, the most effective step in helping you become a fat adapted runner is where you run on empty. That's right, no pre-race meals, no consumption mid-run…nothing. This is in combination with your new high-fat/low-carb healthy eating habits. That's also considering you're not drinking sugary beverages like soda.

Here's the process for running on empty:

1. Wake up early in the morning.
2. Drink a glass of water.
3. Go run.

There's a magnificent beauty in simplicity, wouldn't you agree? You then increase the mileage of your next run which increases the distance you run on empty. That's it! The key to becoming a fat adapted runner is exactly like becoming a long-distance runner: you must progress one run at a time.

To help, I'll provide fat adapted training programs for different distances. Each training program contains one long run every 7 days. Complete each run on empty. Personally, I did not drink water while running; however, whether you consume food or water is a decision you must make on your own.

Below you will find a fat adapted training program for the following distances: 5k, 10k, half-marathon, marathon, and 50k. I recommend you begin one distance behind your current best. For example, if you are a marathon runner, begin with the half-marathon program. Or if you are an ultramarathon runner, begin with the marathon program.

At the end of the book, there is a section for journaling. I recommend taking notes after each run. By reflecting on your progress, you will become more self-aware. Your body is always communicating with you. The more you hear, the more positive changes you can make to improve as a fat adapted runner.

Are you ready? Great! Let's get started. Go ahead and choose a plan on the following pages.

Week	Mon	Tues	Wed	Thu	Fri	Sat	Sun
1	Rest	Rest	Rest	Rest	Rest	Rest	**1.1**
2	Rest	Rest	Rest	Rest	Rest	Rest	**1.2**
3	Rest	Rest	Rest	Rest	Rest	Rest	**1.3**
4	Rest	Rest	Rest	Rest	Rest	Rest	**1.4**
5	Rest	Rest	Rest	Rest	Rest	Rest	**1.6**
6	Rest	Rest	Rest	Rest	Rest	Rest	**1.7**
7	Rest	Rest	Rest	Rest	Rest	Rest	**1.9**
8	Rest	Rest	Rest	Rest	Rest	Rest	**2.1**
9	Rest	Rest	Rest	Rest	Rest	Rest	**1.1**
10	Rest	Rest	Rest	Rest	Rest	Rest	**0.8**
11	Rest	Rest	Rest	Rest	Rest	Rest	**0.4**
12	Rest	Rest	Rest	Rest	Rest	Rest	**5k**

The 5k Fat Adapted Running Formula Training Program ™

*Recommendation: If you've run the 10k distance, start with the 5k training program.

The 10k Fat Adapted Running Formula Training Program ™							
Week	**Mon**	**Tues**	**Wed**	**Thu**	**Fri**	**Sat**	**Sun**
1	Rest	Rest	Rest	Rest	Rest	Rest	**2.25**
2	Rest	Rest	Rest	Rest	Rest	Rest	**2.5**
3	Rest	Rest	Rest	Rest	Rest	Rest	**2.75**
4	Rest	Rest	Rest	Rest	Rest	Rest	**3**
5	Rest	Rest	Rest	Rest	Rest	Rest	**3.25**
6	Rest	Rest	Rest	Rest	Rest	Rest	**3.5**
7	Rest	Rest	Rest	Rest	Rest	Rest	**3.75**
8	Rest	Rest	Rest	Rest	Rest	Rest	**4.25**
9	Rest	Rest	Rest	Rest	Rest	Rest	**2.25**
10	Rest	Rest	Rest	Rest	Rest	Rest	**1.75**
11	Rest	Rest	Rest	Rest	Rest	Rest	**0.75**
12	Rest	Rest	Rest	Rest	Rest	Rest	**10k**

*Recommendation: If you've run the half-marathon distance, start with the 10k training program.

The Half-Marathon Fat Adapted Running Formula Training Program ™							
Week	Mon	Tues	Wed	Thu	Fri	Sat	Sun
1	Rest	Rest	Rest	Rest	Rest	Rest	**4.5**
2	Rest	Rest	Rest	Rest	Rest	Rest	**5**
3	Rest	Rest	Rest	Rest	Rest	Rest	**5.5**
4	Rest	Rest	Rest	Rest	Rest	Rest	**6**
5	Rest	Rest	Rest	Rest	Rest	Rest	**6.5**
6	Rest	Rest	Rest	Rest	Rest	Rest	**7.5**
7	Rest	Rest	Rest	Rest	Rest	Rest	**8**
8	Rest	Rest	Rest	Rest	Rest	Rest	**9**
9	Rest	Rest	Rest	Rest	Rest	Rest	**4.5**
10	Rest	Rest	Rest	Rest	Rest	Rest	**3.5**
11	Rest	Rest	Rest	Rest	Rest	Rest	**1.5**
12	Rest	Rest	Rest	Rest	Rest	Rest	**13.1**

*Recommendation: If you've run the marathon distance, start with the half-marathon training program.

| The Marathon Fat Adapted Running Formula Training Program ™ | | | | | | | |
Week	Mon	Tues	Wed	Thu	Fri	Sat	Sun
1	Rest	Rest	Rest	Rest	Rest	Rest	9
2	Rest	Rest	Rest	Rest	Rest	Rest	10
3	Rest	Rest	Rest	Rest	Rest	Rest	11
4	Rest	Rest	Rest	Rest	Rest	Rest	12
5	Rest	Rest	Rest	Rest	Rest	Rest	13
6	Rest	Rest	Rest	Rest	Rest	Rest	15
7	Rest	Rest	Rest	Rest	Rest	Rest	16
8	Rest	Rest	Rest	Rest	Rest	Rest	18
9	Rest	Rest	Rest	Rest	Rest	Rest	9
10	Rest	Rest	Rest	Rest	Rest	Rest	7
11	Rest	Rest	Rest	Rest	Rest	Rest	3
12	Rest	Rest	Rest	Rest	Rest	Rest	26.2

Recommendation: If you've run the 50k distance, start with the marathon training program.

14

Week	Mon	Tues	Wed	Thu	Fri	Sat	Sun
The 50k Fat Adapted Running Formula Training Program ™							
1	Rest	Rest	Rest	Rest	Rest	Rest	**11**
2	Rest	Rest	Rest	Rest	Rest	Rest	**12**
3	Rest	Rest	Rest	Rest	Rest	Rest	**13**
4	Rest	Rest	Rest	Rest	Rest	Rest	**14**
5	Rest	Rest	Rest	Rest	Rest	Rest	**16**
6	Rest	Rest	Rest	Rest	Rest	Rest	**17**
7	Rest	Rest	Rest	Rest	Rest	Rest	**19**
8	Rest	Rest	Rest	Rest	Rest	Rest	**21**
9	Rest	Rest	Rest	Rest	Rest	Rest	**11**
10	Rest	Rest	Rest	Rest	Rest	Rest	**8**
11	Rest	Rest	Rest	Rest	Rest	Rest	**4**
12	Rest	Rest	Rest	Rest	Rest	Rest	**50k**

Recommendation: If you've run the 50-mile distance or longer, start with the 50k training program.

Now you have a training program for each distance. These are the same programs I used to become fat adapted and they are the same programs that will work for you. Don't let running one day per week discourage you. Indeed, I've run one day per week and reached distances as long as the 100-mile ultramarathon. I explain this method in my book *A Runner's Secret*.

Although you will run one day per week, it doesn't mean your run will be easy. Running on empty is tiring at first, no matter how you frame it. In the beginning, you feel bogged down from limited sugar, but trust that if you slow your pace and keep moving your feet forward, your body will adapt and you will find a way.

As I write this, I've just completed an official 50k race with no food or water—zero intake. Fasting while you run is very possible, you just have to take it slow. Eventually, your body adapts, and now you developed the superpowers of a fat adapted runner. No, it's not always easy. In fact, running on empty can be challenging. There are many temptations to stop and fuel. Especially when running on the road.

Change the Distance in Your Mind

During the process of becoming a fat adapted runner, I left home without supplies. This way I had no option but to finish without fueling. However, I did bring money in case of an emergency. When your supplies are close by, it's much more tempting to hit a store and grab a sports drink. To help, when I'm running on empty and passing a store, I use the following mental strategy…

When I run long distances, it's critical I stay in the present moment, so if I am losing focus, I start breaking the run into sections. Like the run is only as long as my next turn. Each small victory from street corner to street corner helps take my mind away from the incredibly long distance to the end of my run.

How does this apply when running on empty? Well, let's take an extreme example of when I run 31 miles (50k) with no food or water. If I'm on the road running by a store in the later stages of my run, everything in my body tells me to stop for a drink. Instead of trying to hype myself up and run past the store and push through to the end, I just change the distance in my mind.

What do I mean by "*change the distance*"? The answer: I use the same mental strategy as with running to the next street corner. I break the run up into smaller sections, except in this example, the smaller section is only past the store. What I do is focus on an object somewhere down the road from where I am. I then consider that object as the only distance I am now running. It doesn't matter how many miles I have left or how many miles I've run already. The only thing that matters is that point down the road. That's all there is and all there ever was.

Fueling As an Option

Now, I know, running completely on empty can be extreme for some in the beginning. If you must fuel with an external source of energy when following your training program, just hold off on the sugar as long as possible. Also, note the mile of consumption so you can run further without it on your next run. For example, let's say you are using the marathon training program to become fat adapted. On your first run, which is 9 miles, you consume a sports drink at mile 7. Well, on your next run, which is 10 miles, try to go 8 miles without the drink. Your progression is no longer a focus on distance alone, but on the distance you run without external fuel.

Never forget that the human body adapts. Running without water is an adaptation my body has developed. That's why I've even competed in ultramarathons without food or water, but it didn't happen overnight. All of my training runs are now completed on empty. My body doesn't only expect fasting while running, but it craves it. If I go too long without a fasted run, I feel uneasy. It's become so much more than an advantage for running. It now feels like a purification process and that goes for my mind, body, and soul.

Between races and training runs, I've run over 100 ultramarathon distances. Can you imagine how many times I've run on empty? It started with following these programs I developed. As I mentioned, *The Transformation* is where theory becomes fact. It's where you truly begin making progress as a fat adapted runner. Follow this chapter and you will become a fat adapted runner once and for all. Feel free to stay here for a while and really dig into the fat adapted running process. Fine-tune your nutrition, work to cut out grains completely, and progress to further mileage.

Here's What to Do Next...

When you're ready, move onto the next chapter. *The Calibration* is where you dial into your new fat adapted runner body and gain speed through a natural approach. Feel free to use *The Calibration* as much or as little as you like.

Within this chapter, you will learn how to use your heart to become even more efficient at burning fat. I will also provide advice on how to calibrate by feel. These steps will help take your new fat adapted running body to a competitive level by increasing your speed. If anything, it's a way to find a fat burning pace that's right for you. So, read on and begin calibrating.

CHAPTER 6:

The Calibration

Ready to speed up by slowing down? That's what this chapter is all about. It explains how to use your heart rate to become a faster fat adapted runner without a tracking device.

Webster dictionary defines *"calibrate"* as *"to determine, check, or rectify the graduation of something."* That's exactly what you'll be doing in this chapter. You'll find your fat-burning heart rate zone by feel and develop the self-discipline to stay in it. You will also push past your fat-burning heart rate zone to become a faster fat adapted runner.

While running as a fat adapted runner, the idea is to try and keep your heart beats per minute (bpm) low. When you are aware of your heart rate, you now have the potential to learn more about your body. The most obvious observation you will find is how your heart-rate is a direct reflection of how fast you run. Simply stated, the faster you run, the higher your heart rate and the slower you run, the lower your heart rate.

While following *The Calibration*, you'll notice you're becoming a faster fat adapted runner. Eventually, while running, you'll stay in your fat burning heart rate zone while maintaining a faster pace. In other words, your heart will become more efficient.

The idea is to get your heart pumping more blood with each beat. Through heart rate training, your muscles will become more efficient at using the oxygen in your blood. There's plenty of scientific data to support this process. I'll leave that data for the textbooks. For this book's purposes, I am providing a step-by-step guide to achieve results. So keep reading as I explain how to find your fat burning heart-rate zone and use it to become a faster and more efficient fat adapted runner.

You see, I run on feel and prefer running as minimalistically as possible. On the other hand, some use mathematical formulas and tracking devices to become a faster fat adapted runner. So, remember, different methods are for different runners. Either way, give my method a try. It's far less complicated and still provides an avenue for becoming faster with less effort.

So, let's start by slowing down and find your fat-burning heart rate zone, also what I refer to as your *easy* zone.

Take It Easy

It's essential to slow down your pace considerably as you become a fat adapted runner. However, this can be discouraging. You feel like you are losing your speed or losing ground on your next personal best. Running is about growth and progress, but it feels as if you are taking steps in the wrong direction. However, I have a question for you: Have you ever heard the saying *"Two steps forward, one step backward?"* I know, it may sound cliché, but this couldn't be any closer to the truth. It's imperative to keep your body in an aerobic state when becoming fat adapted. The body burns a much greater amount of fat at a lower intensity when performing aerobic activity.

If you remember from *The Foundation*, aerobic literally means *"with oxygen."* It's when you exercise at an easy-to-moderate pace like in long-distance running. When you perform aerobic activity, you're primarily burning fat as fuel. Make a note: aerobic intensity is what you'll use as your fat-burning heart rate zone. When you are running, not breathing heavy, and can still hold a conversation, then you have reached a bpm that will benefit you in becoming a more efficient fat adapted runner.

So now the question becomes: "What's the right amount of aerobic activity for fat adapted running?" At first, I recommend spending 100% of your time in an aerobic state. Then, after your first running program is complete, or whenever your body starts changing, you can step out of the fat-burning heart rate zone. Here is when you will spend approximately 85% of your run at an easy pace, 10% at a moderate pace, and 5% at a fast pace.

In the early stages of the program, run at your fat-burning heart rate zone 100% of the time. You will most likely feel sluggish and tired at the beginning of your fat adapted journey. Considerably slowing down your pace will help your body continue to run, even with the drastic reduction of sugar. Here's a tip: whenever your stomach grumbles, slow down your speed and take shorter steps. Eventually, your body will adjust, and you can pick the pace back up.

Next, continue reading as I talk about speed training. I will explain how to find your *moderate* pace and *fast* pace heart rate zones without a tracker.

Take It Moderate and Fast

As I mentioned, when first practicing fat adapted running, I ran at a low intensity 100% of the time. Once I started feeling the positive effects of burning fat as fuel, I began accepting a slower pace. It wasn't just making my body feel better over long distances, but it was making my body feel better in general. Then add in the elimination of processed foods, and life just felt…great!

The thing is when you first start relying on fat as fuel, your body doesn't like it. You are depriving it of sugar. It has not yet begun to burn fat as fuel efficiently, so it feels tired and weak. Your stomach rumbles and gravity feels heavier. In these circumstances, I would slow down even more. I learned the importance of not paying attention to pace during my transformation period. Your body needs time to adjust.

So, when are you ready to transfer from a 100% easy pace? Well, you can wait until your first fasted fat adapted training program is complete. If you aspire to start sooner, look out for a few signals that you have become fat adapted. Although it's difficult to measure when you've become a fat adapted runner, the way you feel is your best guide. Here are a few good signs…

- Running without carbs no longer causes quick fatigue.
- You can go several hours without eating.
- Skipping a meal doesn't cause a negative mood change.
- Your energy feels steady throughout the day.
- You have no headaches or foggy feelings.

If you feel like you've reached this point, then you've probably reached the tipping point. You have become fat adapted. You can now switch from running 100% of the time in a fat-burning heart rate zone to 85% easy pace, 10% moderate pace, and 5% fast pace. Here's how I feel it out: I run 85% of the time at a pace where I can hold a conversation, 10% in an edgy groove, and 5% in a fast pace, broken up at intervals throughout my run. I don't track my fast pace with a watch. If I did, I would probably be faster and burn fat more efficiently. I prefer running on feel. Less tracking is more motivating for me and my running style, but again, we are all different.

So let's say I'm running for two hours. I know 6 x 1:00-minute sprints spaced out throughout my run will get me there. During these sprints, I find an object in the distance and sprint towards it as fast as possible. As long as the sprint feels about one minute long, I then immediately drop back to an easy pace.

As your heart becomes more efficient, you will run a quicker pace while maintaining a steady heart rate. You can now show up on race day and run with far less sugary foods and supplements. Or you can choose a cleaner path like myself and fuel 100% naturally. Although it's not the fastest method, it sure is the healthiest.

During *The Calibration,* you will face many obstacles that send your heart rate off track. The biggest issue will be hills. How you tackle hills has the potential to shoot your heart rate into a sugar-dependent state. So to help, I will teach you how to run hills as a new fat adapted runner.

Make Hills Disappear

We all have different relationships with hills. They are our best friends for some…and worst enemies for others. One thing we know for certain is this: hills create more resistance.

If you are practicing fat adapted running and want to stay at an easy pace, then place an awareness on every hill. When running uphill, your heart rate will naturally increase if you run at the same pace. So take notice of your speed with each new hill.

Remember—the body burns a much greater amount of fat at a lower intensity. Increasing your pace too much can have an adverse effect in becoming a fat adapted runner. It can create extreme fatigue, making your run more challenging or forcing you to reach for a sugary supplement. Either way, increasing your pace can bring your body closer to sugar dependency and further away from fat adapted.

As I transferred into becoming a fat adapted runner, I took hills slowly. They became less of an obstacle and more of a time for me to sharpen my self-discipline. As much as I wanted to run fast uphill, I knew it would have a negative effect on my progress. So I focused on the big picture, and forced myself to slow down.

Even at a sloth-like pace, sometimes the resistance of the hill still makes it challenging to keep your heart rate down. So, what's the best way to keep your heart rate low when running uphill? Easy: make the hill disappear. Yes, that's right. You can turn a hill into a flat surface.

What do I mean exactly? Well, you can change the overall dynamic of your motion when running uphill. All you need to do is take shorter steps. Similar to shifting a bike to a lower gear, a shorter step requires more revolutions but less energy per revolution. The change in motion can feel as if you're running on flat terrain. In this way, the hills begin to disappear, and you can stay in an easy aerobic state.

Here's What to Do Next...

Now that you have read *The Calibration* and have a clear path to becoming a more efficient fat adapted runner, it's time to apply the work. What discourages some in life is an advantage to others. That's because what you put into life is exactly what you get out. In running, there's no one holding you accountable but yourself.

It's those extra steps you take while feeling discouraged that push you over the top to become fat adapted. It's those runs when you progress a little further on empty while everything in your body *screams* to stop. It's saying "NO" to that piece of bread when the norm is telling you to eat it. It's about having the discipline to stay at a fat-burning pace when your ego tells you to run faster. The persistence in your resilience is what separates fat adapted runners from sugar-dependent runners. Then, soon, your body transforms and becomes the fat adapted machine it was meant to be. Fat begins to melt away, and all your hard work pays off.

Remember—although becoming fat adapted requires an enormous physical effort, it's our mind that powers the body forward. Without the right mentality, quitting becomes easier as your progress slows down and running on empty develops into a more challenging experience.

Here's a tip: do you know how to accomplish any running goal? The answer: *always take one more step*. When you become discouraged, always take one more step. You may be cutting through miles of brush on your path to fat adapted running with no visibility ahead. Chop after chop provides the same result: *more brush*. Here is where some will quit without realizing they were only one chop away from reaching an unstoppable fat adapted running body. To create an unstoppable body takes an unstoppable mind.

So, next and lastly, let's discuss the mental side of the fat adapted running equation. Continue reading as I explain the mental strategies that will help you chop through *The Fat Adapted Running Formula*™ without quitting. The next chapter will help you reach the other side of the running world where the greatest endurance athletes on the planet reside. A place where there are no limits in the sky, and the only barriers that exist are self-created in the mind. Next, we will discuss *The Glue* that bonds the entire program together. *The Glue* of the program is the fat adapted running mindset.

CHAPTER 7:

The Glue

I t's time to construct an unbreakable mental edge to guide you through *The Fat Adapted Running Formula™*. By following *The Glue*, you'll hold yourself together when times get tough along your fat adapted running journey. If you feel discouraged, come back to this chapter and reread it as many times as need be. In fact, I highly recommend reading this chapter often. Reading *The Glue* first thing in the morning sets the stage for your entire day. It provides continuous encouragement to leverage the good days and to continue moving forward during the bad days. So, start; take a leap of faith.

Take a Leap of Faith

In running, sometimes you just have to take a leap of faith. You sign up for a further distance, show up on race day, and go for it.

Standing at the starting line of a 200-mile ultramarathon, I had no idea if I could cover such an extraordinary distance. Then I thought if a few other people in the world could do it, then why not me?

So why not you? Sure, you may not be planning on running 200 miles, but the same principle applies when it comes to fat adapted running. You must begin, have faith in the process, and most importantly, have faith in yourself. Understand that the process of fat adaptation does not occur without stress. If you want to run further and take advantage of fat adapted running, then you'll need to keep pushing your limits. There is no other way.

Being able to run 31 miles (50k) without food or water didn't happen right away. I pushed the limits a little more each week. If I didn't constantly push the boundaries, I would have never made it that far. Never forget these words: *when you step outside of your comfort zone, growth is a guarantee.*

Here's the point: if you sign up for a longer race then you typically run, you will allow yourself to become fat adapted more quickly. Don't get lost in the generality of running. Set a clear and precise goal to run a further distance. This way you can take your fat adapted running to the next level in correspondence with that particular distance.

For example, it wasn't until I trained for 50 and 100-mile ultramarathons that it was possible for me to run 31 miles (50k) without food or water. How would I ever have developed the mindset for doing so if I couldn't even run the distance while externally fueling? For you, it may be a half marathon to a marathon, or a marathon to a 50k. Whatever the distance, know that we are either growing or dying, becoming stronger or weaker, moving forward or backward. Growth is the way of life. Know that your fat metabolism is either getting more efficient or less efficient. Nothing in life is static. Let's face it, if we are not progressing, we are digressing.

Consider your bones. To the eye, they seem hard and solid and are many times thought of as a static structure. Yet the skeletal system is dynamic, with many different functions. Bones are living tissue, and despite their hard and solid appearance; they constantly change throughout our lifetime. When you place a constant demand on your bones, they grow back stronger and denser, adapting to their new environment. This would be similar to the callus on our hands or the growth of our muscles. Just like the calluses we develop on our body, we can develop calluses on our mind, metaphorically speaking.

Running with no food or water wasn't just difficult physically. It was a mental journey. Distinguishing between hunger and starvation is difficult to comprehend at times. So as you become a more proficient fat adapted runner, you will have to reach further and further past your comfort zone. This will take an extraordinary mindset, a mindset you will develop one day at a time.

Before I start fueling on race day, I think to myself, "Have I started suffering yet?" If the answer is "No," then I keep moving forward. The endurance you develop from running derives directly from the struggles you experience.

Fat adapted running is a process with no definitive end. It's not like a race where there is a finish line. As you progress, you notice changes like being able to run further with no food or not craving that piece of chocolate. You begin to feel more balanced throughout your day. Yet in the beginning, fat adapted running can create difficulties. Here's the problem: for some, without a finish line, the process of becoming fat adapted is discouraging. You have to trust the process, and most importantly…trust yourself and enjoy the journey.

Enjoy the Journey

Fat adapted running is a journey. Yes, there will be arrivals like the first time you run 10 miles on empty or the first time you run without feeling sluggish. Know that these arrivals come and go in a fraction of a second. What you really experience are all the small steps you took to become fat adapted. It's not about finally running that race without needing a gel or the 20 lbs you dropped off your racing weight. It's about the 16 weeks of training while running on empty and the months you went without eating a single piece of bread.

That's why fat adapted runners lose weight so well. It's because you bring your awareness away from weight loss and focus on the actual fat adapted running process itself. You get to a point where you literally become excited to do things like fast and cut out processed foods. The reward is no longer extrinsic, like how you look in the mirror. It becomes more intrinsic, as you're using fat burning as a tool to become a better runner.

So if you are passionate enough about running, as you run more, you'll become leaner automatically. Weight loss becomes a reciprocal of your passion for running. By focusing on the journey of fat adapted running, what you're doing is training yourself to stay in the present moment.

Stay in the Present Moment

When transitioning into a fat adapted runner, there will be times you won't want to go on. It's much easier to give in and reach for that sugary drink, snack, or meal replacement bar. It's tempting to bring along a handful of gels. I know…I've been there myself. Fat adapted running is my lifestyle.

To help, when becoming fat adapted, just like running extreme distances, it's critical to learn how to anchor into the present moment. Know that when you find enjoyment in your journey, staying in the present moment will come easier. For most, the present moment hardly exists, as we become so caught up in our past and future that we never take a second to be still to acknowledge it. As an ultramarathon runner who runs for 100 miles at a time, I've developed this skill, but it's not something I've mastered, and it's not my goal to master it. For me, that's a journey in itself.

It's easy to get caught focusing on the past; that's how most identify themselves—it's who they are, and the future is where people want to go, since they believe that's where they'll be free of their problems. Here's the dilemma: as you work toward that future place, even if you were to arrive there, you would still be looking further into the future. It's a forward way of thinking. Sure, this mindset can serve us to reach new goals and motivate ourselves, but the key is to use it as a tool, not live in the future.

If you stay in the present moment—which separates yourself from the mind, instead of being your *thoughts,* you are the *observer* of thought, you are the *awareness*—you find the freedom you've been searching for all along. Because right now, what troubles do you have? In the present moment, your future troubles and past troubles don't exist. Plus, this helps align you with your authentic self. When you can be yourself 100%, there's no better freedom in the world. This freedom eliminates conflicts from within.

So understand the following: it's not about forgetting the past or present, it's more about using them as a tool rather than allowing your mind to wander while you run. By tapping into the present moment, you can keep moving your feet, even when you're sluggish at the beginning of fat adapted running. Now you can say "NO" to that dessert when your mouth is watering from sugar withdrawal, then walk out the door and run further each week on empty.

Enjoying the journey will keep you in the present moment, and if you practice focusing on your breathing, placing an awareness on your five senses, and being grateful, you will stay there longer. It will become easier to fight the urge of doing something that will harm your progressive journey into fat adapted running.

The fact is, as endurance runners, especially those becoming fat adapted, learning to stay in the present moment is advantageous. It will not just help you through your transformation phase, but it has the potential to transform your life. If you practice it long and hard enough, one day…you'll WAKE UP and realize you've been sleeping all along.

Taking a leap of faith, enjoying the journey, and staying in the present moment are the ingredients that make up *The Glue*. As you can see, it's your mind that holds the entire program together.

Here's What to Do Next…

Now that you have read *The Glue* and know how to apply it to your training, you have everything you need to become a fat adapted runner.

With that, continue reading as we wrap things up and I provide my secret tip to becoming an elite fat adapted runner. A fat adapted runner who not only has run ultramarathons with no food or water, but one who has turned fasted running into a craving from within. I don't force my body to run on empty...my body now *needs* it.

CONCLUSION:

Welcome Home

I reached the 100-mile ultra distance before becoming fat adapted. It was just a lot more involved. The insane amount of sugar intake from grinding out mile after mile not only destroyed my stomach, it drained me mentally. Today, being able to leave my house with zero supplies for any distance less than 40 miles feels super-natural. It's convenient and it provides an increased level of freedom.

...and maybe best yet, fasting for the body is *food for the soul*. When you run on empty and take it to the limit, you find a deeper connection between yourself and your "higher self." Whatever your beliefs, running on empty is a constant means of renewing yourself spiritually.

Fat adapted running is a path not only to better your running and lose weight, but you get in touch with something more profound. You get in touch with something much more meaningful. Fasting as a fat adapted runner and pushing it to ultra distances will make you feel more connected. A connection deeper than what you can see, one of universal proportions that cannot be verbalized.

As I like to say, during a 100-mile ultramarathon, you run the first 50% with your *body*, the second 40% with your *mind*, and the last 10% with your *soul*. Fat adapted running is running while fasted, and fasting strengthens the soul. So when you reach that last 10% of your race as a fat adapted runner, you're now well prepared. That last 10% becomes no longer what you do, it becomes who you are, and you blow through those last miles like you were born to run them.

Welcome to fat adaptation…*the fuel for the soul of human endurance.*

So with that, I'd like to thank you from the bottom of my heart for allowing me to serve you in your fat adapted running journey. As you begin down your path, I will now offer you my greatest tip of all. This has not only helped me run 40 miles on empty, it's how I've run 200 miles in a single race.

My secret tip: I never race against another person, nor do I race against myself. I LET GO. I eliminate the resistance from within and allow my spirit to move me forward.

This life is so much more than we could ever imagine. No one has the answers for you, as every answer is already within you. It's within your heart and we all have an intuitive compass to get us there. It's the same intuition that told you to start running and the same one that told you to read this book.

If *love* is the highest expression of the human soul, then by letting go of egoistic traits like resentment, envy, jealousy, and whatever else is causing resistance from within, you're allowing your true self to shine through. You allow love to fill every crack of your broken being, and that's a type of energy that cannot be restrained, because that energy is infinite.

…and with that, any distance is possible for any fat adapted runner.

When running, it's not about finding a new you, it's about letting more of the real you surface. Running strips away internal resistance and lets your light shine through, especially from a fasted state.

This philosophy has enabled me to take fat adapted running to extraordinary levels. When you believe in something infinitely bigger than yourself, fat adapted running isn't really all that difficult…is it?

So how will you know when you have become fat adapted?

Simple: when you no longer need to ask the question. When the shift occurs, you'll know…and slowly you will develop a sense of infinite possibilities. The feeling will come from within, just like your new way of burning fuel.

Thank you, and enjoy your new home within the fat adapted running world.

JOURNAL:

Write It Down

Several times throughout *The Fat Adapted Running Formula*™, I mention listening to your body. Pay close attention to how your body responds to new changes, especially during your training programs.

The journal section is for developing a new writing practice. By reflecting on your progress, you are focusing your attention as you apply your new fat adapted running strategies. By taking notes on what's working, and what is not, you will only further strengthen your path to progress.

Ask yourself different questions. For example: What time did I begin my run? Did I stick to the plan? How far did I run without external fuel? At what mile did my body slow down? Was I prepared enough? How did my body feel before and after my run? What can I do better? What actions inspire me most? What have I learned that will help me for my next run?

As time goes on, journaling will increase your awareness. Listening to your body will become a habit as you adventure through The Fat Adapted Running Formula™. Journaling will ensure your success as an efficient fat adapted runner. So, write it down!

The 5k Fat Adapted Running Formula Training Journal

WEEK 1: Post-Run Reflection

_____

_____

_____

_____

_____

_____

_____

_____

_____

WEEK 2: Post-Run Reflection

_____

_____

_____

_____

_____

_____

_____

_____

_____

WEEK 3: Post-Run Reflection

_____

_____

_____

_____

_____

_____

_____

_____

_____

_____

WEEK 4: Post-Run Reflection

_____

_____

_____

_____

_____

_____

_____

_____

_____

_____

WEEK 5: Post-Run Reflection

_____

_____

_____

_____

_____

_____

_____

_____

_____

_____

WEEK 6: Post-Run Reflection

_____

_____

_____

_____

_____

_____

_____

_____

_____

_____

WEEK 7: Post-Run Reflection

_____

_____

_____

_____

_____

_____

_____

_____

_____

_____

WEEK 8: Post-Run Reflection

_____

_____

_____

_____

_____

_____

_____

_____

_____

_____

WEEK 9: Post-Run Reflection

_____

_____

_____

_____

_____

_____

_____

_____

_____

_____

WEEK 10: Post-Run Reflection

_____

_____

_____

_____

_____

_____

_____

_____

_____

_____

WEEK 11: Post-Run Reflection

_____

_____

_____

_____

_____

_____

_____

_____

_____

_____

WEEK 12: Post-Run Reflection

_____

_____

_____

_____

_____

_____

_____

_____

_____

_____

The Half-Marathon Fat Adapted Running Formula Training Journal

WEEK 1: Post-Run Reflection

_____

_____

_____

_____

_____

_____

_____

_____

_____

WEEK 2: Post-Run Reflection

_____

_____

_____

_____

_____

_____

_____

_____

_____

WEEK 3: Post-Run Reflection

_____

_____

_____

_____

_____

_____

_____

_____

_____

_____

WEEK 4: Post-Run Reflection

_____

_____

_____

_____

_____

_____

_____

_____

_____

_____

_____

WEEK 5: Post-Run Reflection

_____

_____

_____

_____

_____

_____

_____

_____

_____

WEEK 6: Post-Run Reflection

_____

_____

_____

_____

_____

_____

_____

_____

_____

_____

WEEK 7: Post-Run Reflection

_____

_____

_____

_____

_____

_____

_____

_____

_____

_____

WEEK 8: Post-Run Reflection

_____

_____

_____

_____

_____

_____

_____

_____

_____

_____

WEEK 9: Post-Run Reflection

_____

_____

_____

_____

_____

_____

_____

_____

_____

_____

WEEK 10: Post-Run Reflection

_____

_____

_____

_____

_____

_____

_____

_____

_____

_____

_____

WEEK 11: Post-Run Reflection

_____

_____

_____

_____

_____

_____

_____

_____

_____

_____

WEEK 12: Post-Run Reflection

_____

_____

_____

_____

_____

_____

_____

_____

_____

_____

The Marathon Fat Adapted Running Formula Training Journal

WEEK 1: Post-Run Reflection

_____

_____

_____

_____

_____

_____

_____

_____

_____

WEEK 2: Post-Run Reflection

_____

_____

_____

_____

_____

_____

_____

_____

_____

WEEK 3: Post-Run Reflection

_____

_____

_____

_____

_____

_____

_____

_____

_____

_____

WEEK 4: Post-Run Reflection

_____

_____

_____

_____

_____

_____

_____

_____

_____

_____

WEEK 5: Post-Run Reflection

_____

_____

_____

_____

_____

_____

_____

_____

_____

_____

WEEK 6: Post-Run Reflection

_____

_____

_____

_____

_____

_____

_____

_____

_____

_____

WEEK 7: Post-Run Reflection

_____

_____

_____

_____

_____

_____

_____

_____

_____

_____

WEEK 8: Post-Run Reflection

_____

_____

_____

_____

_____

_____

_____

_____

_____

_____

WEEK 9: Post-Run Reflection

_____

_____

_____

_____

_____

_____

_____

_____

_____

_____

WEEK 10: Post-Run Reflection

_____

_____

_____

_____

_____

_____

_____

_____

_____

_____

_____

WEEK 11: Post-Run Reflection

_____

_____

_____

_____

_____

_____

_____

_____

_____

_____

WEEK 12: Post-Run Reflection

_____

_____

_____

_____

_____

_____

_____

_____

_____

_____

The 50k Fat Adapted Running Formula Training Journal

WEEK 1: Post-Run Reflection

_____

_____

_____

_____

_____

_____

_____

_____

_____

WEEK 2: Post-Run Reflection

_____

_____

_____

_____

_____

_____

_____

_____

_____

WEEK 3: Post-Run Reflection

_____

_____

_____

_____

_____

_____

_____

_____

WEEK 4: Post-Run Reflection

_____

_____

_____

_____

_____

_____

_____

_____

_____

WEEK 5: Post-Run Reflection

_____

_____

_____

_____

_____

_____

_____

_____

_____

_____

WEEK 6: Post-Run Reflection

_____

_____

_____

_____

_____

_____

_____

_____

_____

_____

_____

WEEK 7: Post-Run Reflection

_____

_____

_____

_____

_____

_____

_____

_____

_____

_____

WEEK 8: Post-Run Reflection

_____

_____

_____

_____

_____

_____

_____

_____

_____

_____

WEEK 9: Post-Run Reflection

_____

_____

_____

_____

_____

_____

_____

_____

_____

_____

WEEK 10: Post-Run Reflection

_____

_____

_____

_____

_____

_____

_____

_____

_____

_____

_____

WEEK 11: Post-Run Reflection

_____

_____

_____

_____

_____

_____

_____

_____

_____

_____

WEEK 12: Post-Run Reflection

_____

_____

_____

_____

_____

_____

_____

_____

_____

_____

Printed in Great Britain
by Amazon

38464887R00068